Understanding the World's Greatest Structures: Science and Innovation from Antiquity to Modernity

Stephen Ressler, Ph.D.

THE GREAT COURSES®

PUBLISHED BY:

THE GREAT COURSES
Corporate Headquarters
4840 Westfields Boulevard, Suite 500
Chantilly, Virginia 20151-2299
Phone: 1-800-832-2412
Fax: 703-378-3819
www.thegreatcourses.com

Stephen Ressler, Ph.D.

Professor of Civil Engineering
United States Military Academy at West Point

Colonel Stephen Ressler is a Professor of Civil Engineering at the United States Military Academy at West Point. He earned a Bachelor of Science degree from West Point, Master's and Ph.D. degrees in Civil Engineering from Lehigh University, and a Master of Strategic Studies degree from the U.S. Army War College. He is a registered professional engineer in the commonwealth of Virginia.

Professor Ressler was commissioned as an officer in the Army Corps of Engineers in 1979. Since then, he has served in a variety of military engineering assignments in the United States, Europe, and Central Asia. He has been a member of the West Point faculty for 19 years, teaching a variety of courses in engineering mechanics, structural analysis, structural design, construction management, and civil engineering professional practice. In 2007, he deployed to Afghanistan to develop a civil engineering program for the newly created National Military Academy of Afghanistan in Kabul. In that capacity, he designed the academy's civil engineering curriculum, hired its first cohort of Afghan faculty, and developed 2 laboratory facilities.

Professor Ressler has focused his scholarly work and professional service in the area of engineering education. He has written more than 80 scholarly papers on teaching techniques, faculty development, curriculum assessment, engineering outreach to primary and secondary schools, engineering accreditation, and information technology. His work has earned 7 Best Paper Awards from the American Society for Engineering Education.

Professor Ressler is the creator and director of the West Point Bridge Design Contest (see http://bridgecontest.usma.edu), a nationwide Internet-based competition that has introduced engineering to more than 50,000 middle school and high school students since 2001. He is also a developer and principal instructor for the Excellence in Civil Engineering Education (ExCEEd) Teaching Workshop, a landmark faculty-development program sponsored by the American Society of Civil Engineers (ASCE). The workshop has provided rigorous teacher training to more than 500 civil engineering faculty members from more than 200 colleges and universities over the past 12 years.

Professor Ressler has won numerous prestigious national awards. From ASCE, he received the President's Medal and the ExCEEd Leadership Award. ASCE also named him a Distinguished Member in 2005. From the American Society for Engineering Education, he received the George K. Wadlin Distinguished Service Award, the Distinguished Educator Award, and the Dow Outstanding New Faculty Award. He also received the Society of American Military Engineers' Bliss Medal for Outstanding Contributions to Engineering Education; the American Association of Engineering Societies' Norm Augustine Award for Outstanding Achievement in Engineering Communications; the Premier Award for Excellence in Engineering Education Courseware; and the EDUCOM Medal for application of information technology in education.

Professor Ressler was one of *Engineering News Record*'s "Top 25 Newsmakers Who Served Construction" in 2000. Most recently, he received ASCE's highest award—the Outstanding Projects and Leaders (OPAL) Award for 2011. The OPAL Award is presented to only 5 of ASCE's 140,000 members each year. ∎

Table of Contents

Table of Contents

Table of Contents

Understanding the World's Greatest Structures: Science and Innovation from Antiquity to Modernity

Scope:

What makes a structure—a building, bridge, or tower—great? The phrase "great structure" might bring to mind structures famous for their age, their size, their beauty, or all three: Egypt's pyramids, France's Gothic cathedrals, or New York's skyscrapers, just to name a few. But from an engineer's perspective, greatness is not just a matter of aesthetics. In fact, most engineers agree with the pronouncement by Vitruvius, a 1st-century B.C. Roman architect-engineer. To be considered great, Vitruvius said in his treatise *De architectura*, a construction must be exemplary in its form, function, or structure. In this course, we will not only study the principles of form, function, and structure—the "why"—that made these particular structures great; we will also look at the mathematical and mechanical principles—the "how"—of their construction; after all, the only thing more awe inspiring than seeing a great structure is understanding the complex and beautiful principles behind its construction.

The course is roughly divided into 3 parts. In the first part, we'll look at the physical laws that underlie the engineering of great structures. We will look at some of the math, but mostly we will learn to use free-body diagrams the way modern engineers do to trace the flow of forces through a construction. With those tools in hand, we'll embark on the second part of the course, studying the 6 basic types of structural members—arches, beams, cables, columns, tension members, and trusses—that are the basic parts of any structure. We'll learn about how each of these members behaves under load and how it contributes to the overall stability of a structure—or lack thereof. In this part, we'll also look at various construction materials—from early uses of wood, stone, and mud brick to modern materials like steel and reinforced concrete—and how each is particularly suited to use in different structural members.

Finally, the third and longest part of the course will be spent looking at the world's greatest structures themselves, as well as some less-successful structures that nonetheless contributed to the development of engineering knowledge. We'll start with the Pyramids at Giza—some of the oldest surviving structures that can legitimately be called works of engineering—and other great works of the ancient and classical Mediterranean world. We'll look at how and why the arch became the signature of the great architectural works of Roman civilization and how they used this structural form to such amazing effect. We'll examine the great cathedrals of Europe, from the great Romanesque basilicas through the stunning stone skeletons of the Gothic period to the brilliant innovations of Renaissance engineers. Next, we'll learn about the challenge of bridge building and the many ingenious solutions engineers have developed for spanning great distances with safety, economy, and beauty. Then we'll turn to the phenomenon of skyscrapers—the innovations that made them possible and the amazing ways they met the challenge of attaining great height. At last, we'll look at perhaps the most underappreciated feature of any great structure, the roof, and how techniques both new and old have created myriad, beautiful ways for achieving the deceptively simple goal of shelter.

The course wraps up with a final lecture on putting all of this knowledge to use, giving you a chance to test your skills in analyzing structures. My hope is that when you finish this course, you will have a new appreciation of the wonderful structures all around you, from the simplest to the most complex—an appreciation born not only of aesthetic appreciation but of a deep understanding of the principles that made them possible. ∎

Learning to See and Understand Structure
Lecture 1

> Singing my days,
> Singing the great achievements of the present
> Singing the strong, light works of engineers.
>   — Walt Whitman, "Passage to India"

The "strong, light works of engineers" that Walt Whitman celebrates are the buildings, bridges, and towers that surround us, and as he suggests, the best of them should be celebrated as exemplary human achievements, some of which define the eras in which they were built. But to celebrate them, we need to understand them. What makes a building, bridge, or tower great? In his book *De architectura*, 1st-century B.C. Roman architect-engineer Vitruvius said great constructions showed exemplary **form**, **function**, or **structure**. Exemplary form means a sophisticated arrangement of space and harmonious proportions. Exemplary function is a measure of a structure's practical usefulness or cultural significance. Exemplary structure refers to constructions of unprecedented size or innovative techniques that influenced structural **engineering** for years or decades to come.

Let's look at New York's Brooklyn Bridge—one of the few structures almost all experts agree is exemplary—and observe how form, function, and structure play out. Its function is obvious—to span the East River and link Brooklyn and Manhattan—but today its form is what captivates us. The form of the Brooklyn Bridge is certainly beautiful: the graceful curve of cables, the solidity of towers, the intricate web of stiffening trusses. But beyond the aesthetic, these features are a direct reflection of the scientific principles underlying the bridge's design. They are, in a word, structure—a system of **load**-carrying elements that causes the bridge to stand up. Each element of the form of the Brooklyn Bridge serves a structural purpose based on mathematical principles.

What does it take to see structure in a building, bridge, or tower? Generally, the prominence of the structure in any constructed work depends on how demanding the structural requirements are. The more demanding the requirements, the more visible the structure is to the casual observer. There are only three kinds of structural demand: attaining a great height; spanning a great distance; and (particularly in modern structures) achieving "lightness"—that is, using the absolute minimum of material necessary to carry loads safely.

With a bridge, seeing structure is quite easy, so we'll look at a lot of them throughout the course. Bridge design is dominated by the structural concern of spanning a distance, with aesthetics considered at a distant second, if at all. And yet the very shapes, proportions, and arrangement of a bridge's structural elements may be what make it visually compelling. A tower is usually intended to be visually prominent in its environment—think of the way a Gothic cathedral dominates the skyline of an old European city— but its function is still fundamentally structural: to elevate something to a great height. So while a tower's designer generally pays more attention to aesthetics than a bridge's designer does, a tower's structure still tends to be quite evident. With buildings, the principal functions are to enclose space

and to facilitate use of that space. Its functions are performed by many nonstructural subsystems—windows, interior walls, ceilings, lighting, and so forth. Therefore, its structure is often understated or hidden from view entirely and is more difficult to discern, but lack of visibility doesn't mean that structure is not important.

Now that we know something about seeing structure, what does it take to understand structure? First, you need to know some engineering mechanics—the fundamental scientific principles governing the 6 basic load-carrying elements: **tension members**, **columns**, **beams**, **trusses**, **cables**, and **arches**. We'll see how those basic elements work through examining their application in some of the world's great structures. Second, you need to learn to view a building, bridge, or tower as a **structural system**—that is, an interconnected assembly of structural elements that transmit load safely from element to element and finally into the ground. The third aspect of structural understanding is historical context—an appreciation for the engineering tools, materials, and technologies that were available when the structure was designed and built.

© iStockphoto/Thinkstock.

The form of the Brooklyn Bridge is certainly beautiful, but beyond the aesthetic, these features are a direct reflection of the scientific principles underlying the bridge's design.

5

From prehistoric times to the present day, the development of engineering design can be viewed in terms of two broad periods. First was the era of **empirical** design, from about 2500 B.C. to the Renaissance. Throughout this period, design was based entirely on experience with previous structures, sometimes guided by philosophical or geometric principles, but never by true science. Starting in the 17th century, the era of science-based design emerged from the discoveries of the Age of Reason. By the mid-1800s, the scientific methods of designing structures were fully established. They continue today, greatly enhanced by modern computer technology.

What the great structures of the empirical era show us is that science is not actually essential to engineering. The very best empirical engineers worked from a keen qualitative sense of structural principles, even if they were ignorant of the quantitative methods. But science can still help us understand structure more broadly, more deeply, and more efficiently. So science is where we'll begin. ■

Important Terms

arch: A structural element that, because of its shape and support configuration, carries load primarily in compression.

beam: A structural element that is subjected to transverse loading and carries load in bending.

cable: A flexible structural element that carries load entirely in tension and changes its shape in response to the applied loading.

column: A structural element that carries load primarily in compression; also called a compression member.

compression: An internal force that causes a structural element to shorten.

empirical: Based on experience, observation, or experiment.

engineering: The application of math, science, and technology to create a system, component, or process that meets a human need.

force: A push or a pull characterized by a magnitude and a direction. The magnitude of a force is measured in pounds in the U.S. system of units and in Newtons in the International System of units.

form: Appearance, reflected in physical features like shape, scale, proportion, and ornament.

function: Purpose; how something is used by people.

load: An external force acting on a structure.

structural system: An assembly of interconnected structural elements that transmits load from its point of application to the ground.

structure: The load-carrying elements of a building, bridge, or tower.

tension: An internal force that causes a structural element to elongate.

tension member: A structural element that carries load primarily in tension (i.e., by elongating).

truss: A structure consisting of elements arranged in interconnected triangles. These elements carry load primarily in tension or compression.

Suggested Reading

Billington, *The Tower and the Bridge*, chaps. 1 and 5.

Cowan et al., *The World's Greatest Buildings*, p. 11–17.

Gordon, *Structures*, chap. 1.

Salvadori, *Why Buildings Stand Up*, chap. 10.

Note: Answers to all questions marked with asterisks can be found beginning on page 125.

1. Can you provide an example of a great structure that exhibits exemplary form? One that exhibits exemplary function? One that exhibits exemplary structure?

2. Do you think the Washington Monument is a great structure? Can you also see reasons for taking the opposite point of view?

3. Do you think the International Space Station is a great structure?

4. Can you identify each of the 6 basic structural element types—tension member, beam, column, truss, arch, and cable—in structures you have seen or visited recently?

5. What is the relationship between innovative structure and historical context?

6. What are some important differences between the great structures of antiquity and the great structures of today?

The Science of Structure—Forces in Balance
Lecture 2

An understanding of scientific principles allows us to understand and even to design any structure, even if we have no experience with that structure previously. And this is true even for the empirically designed structures of the ancient, medieval, and Renaissance eras, because the science is always there, manifested in the actual behavior of the physical structure.

S ome 4,500 years of empirical design produced many magnificent structures without the aid of any scientific methods at all; nonetheless, when we compare ancient and modern structures, we can't help but recognize that science-based design has opened up vast new realms of structural possibility. Today's engineers still refer to past experience but aren't bound by precedent; they can work with any conceivable structural configuration. They can model structures mathematically, predict how they will respond to loads, and build the structure to carry those loads safely and efficiently. In effect, scientific tools allow modern engineers to predict the future with confidence, even if that future bears very little resemblance to the present or the past. The result is the potential for structures of far greater size and complexity.

Engineering mechanics is the branch of the physical sciences that deals with the effects of a force acting on a **body**. A body is simply a physical object, and a force is a push or a pull applied to an object. Force always has both magnitude and direction. Magnitude is typically expressed in pounds or tons in the United States and Newtons in countries that use the metric system. Everywhere, force is represented with an arrow on a diagram.

Structural analysis always begins with external forces, which include 2 principal loads: **dead loads** (which are permanent) and **live loads** (which vary in force and magnitude). The dead load is mostly the weight of the structure itself; the live loads might be people and objects inside and on top of it, the pressure of wind against it, and so forth. Loads cause **reactions**, an opposite external force that develops at a structure's **supports**—that is, its foundations. **Internal forces** are caused by external forces but occur within the individual structural elements. The 2 principal internal forces are tension and compression. For example, when you bend a straight beam, the inside of the curve is compressed and the outside is stretched (i.e., made tense).

Stress is the measure of the intensity of internal forces. Stress is distributed over the entire cross-section of a member and is expressed as force per area—for example, pounds per square inch or Newtons per square meter. The **strength** of any building material is defined in terms of characteristic values of stress; for example, a standard grade of structural steel fails at a stress of 36,000 pounds per square inch (psi). To evaluate the performance of some material, engineers compare the expected stress against the material's strength. If stress is greater than strength, the material will fail; if stress is less than strength, the structure can carry loads safely. This evaluation is the ultimate goal of structural analysis.

> **The principle of equilibrium is, without question, the most important concept in all of engineering mechanics.**

The principle of **equilibrium** is, without question, the most important concept in all of engineering mechanics. First formulated by Flemish mathematician Simon Stevin in 1586, its most famous form is **Isaac Newton's first law of motion**: An object at rest remains at rest unless acted on by an unbalanced force. A structure is in equilibrium, therefore, when the force pulling it in one direction is balanced by a push in the opposite direction. But because live loads change all the time, a structure has to be able to compensate and create reactions that rebalance an unbalanced force. Because structures are subject to forces from just about any direction, the designing engineer has to consider each force independently to ensure the structure can maintain equilibrium.

Forces can change in magnitude, as, for example, when the downward force of snow on the deck is added to the dead load of a bridge. They can also change in position, as when a train moves from one end of the bridge to another. A change in position doesn't change the magnitude of the force on the whole bridge, but it does change the magnitude of the force on each element of the bridge. For example, a train resting in the middle of a bridge exerts a downward force on both ends of the bridge equally. But if the train were to move toward one end of the bridge, that end would be bearing a greater amount of the force. An off-center force like this causes a tendency to rotate in a structure. We call this tendency the **moment of a force** and calculate it as force times distance. When the load on a structure moves, the moment creates a counterbalancing moment in the supports. So another condition for equilibrium is a balance of moments as well as balance of forces.

The mathematical shorthand for equilibrium is $\sum F_x = 0$, $\sum F_y = 0$, and $\sum M_p = 0$, where $\sum F$ is the sum of the forces in the horizontal (x) or vertical (y) direction and $\sum M$ is the sum of the moments at any point p on the body. If a body is in equilibrium, the sum of all forces acting on the body must equal zero. Engineers use these equations to predict the response of a structure to loads, but the principle of equilibrium also has important implications beyond external forces, as we will soon see. ■

Important Terms

body: A physical object.

dead load: A load that is permanent and unchanging. Dead load includes the weight of the structure itself, plus any nonstructural elements that are permanently attached to the structure.

equilibrium: A condition in which all forces acting on a body are in balance. If a body is not moving (or is moving at a constant velocity), then it is in equilibrium.

free-body diagram: A graphical problem-solving tool showing a body, isolated from its surroundings, annotated with all forces acting on that body.

internal force: The force generated within a structural element in response to external forces. An internal force can be either tension or compression.

live load: A load that varies in both magnitude and location. Live loads include occupancy, traffic, wind, snow, and earthquake loads.

mechanics: The study of forces acting on bodies.

moment of a force: The tendency of a force to cause rotation about a point.

Newton's first law: A body at rest tends to remain at rest, unless it is acted on by an unbalanced force.

reaction: An external force that occurs at a support to keep a structure or structural element in equilibrium.

strength: The largest stress a material can withstand before failing.

stress: The intensity of internal force measured in terms of force per unit area (e.g., pounds per square inch).

support: A physical connection between a structure and its surroundings.

Suggested Reading

Riley, Sturges, and Morris, *Statics and Mechanics of Materials*, chaps. 2, 3, 5, and 6.

Salvadori, *Why Buildings Stand Up*, chap. 5.

Timoshenko, *History of Strength of Materials*.

1. Draw a free-body diagram of the diving board pictured below. What are the directions of the reaction forces at points A and B?*

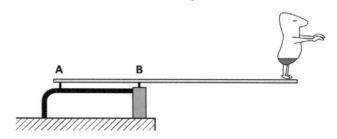

2. To practice what we learned about applying the principle of equilibrium, let's return to the Chouteau Bridge model, this time with a live load of 5 pounds shown below. The bridge itself weighs 2 pounds. What are the reactions at the supports?*

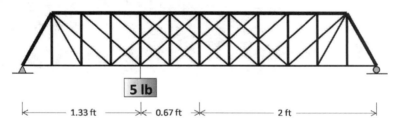

3. Why is it harder to stand on one foot than on two? Explain, using free body diagrams and the principle of equilibrium.*

4. The structure pictured below is a lift bridge located in Delft, Holland. The diagram shows how the span can be raised to allow boats to use the canal below. To lift the bridge deck, a small winch pulls on a lightweight cable, which rotates the lifting arm. How can such a heavy structure be moved by such a small force?*

Photo Courtesy of Dr. Stephen Ressler

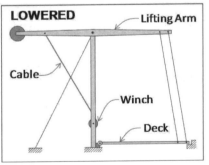

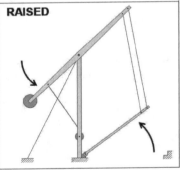

14

Internal Forces, Stress, and Strength
Lecture 3

The stress-strain curve tells us almost everything we need to know about a material's mechanical properties and about its suitability for a particular structural task. Think of the stress-strain curve as the fingerprint of an engineering material and you're pretty well along the way to understanding why it's so valuable to us.

Much of what we know about the strength of an engineering material is gleaned from a very simple laboratory test, the simple tension test: A specimen of the material is slowly stretched by a machine until it breaks. The historical development of this all-important laboratory experiment is a large part of the history of science-based design itself and tells us a lot about the key concepts of structural analysis.

Leonardo da Vinci performed a number of very well-conceived mechanics experiments, including a forerunner to today's simple tension test. His conclusions, however, were a bit off the mark. He concluded, for example, that the strength of iron wire depends on its length; that idea was disproven by none other than Galileo Galilei. Galileo published the world's first comprehensive scientific study of the mechanics of materials in 1638: *Two New Sciences*. His experiments established the fact that the strength of a structural element is independent of its length, disproving Leonardo's assertions, but more importantly, he showed that the strength of a member in tension depends on its **cross-sectional area**—that is, the area of the 2-dimensional shape formed by cutting through the object perpendicular to its long axis. The **cross-section** of a cylinder, for example, is a circle; its cross-sectional area therefore is πr^2. This means that a member with a cross-sectional area of 10 in^2 is twice as strong as a member with a cross-sectional area of 5 in^2 that is made of the same material.

Around 1650, English scientist Robert Hooke took Leonardo's and Galileo's experiments a crucial step farther: Rather than simply determining the breaking point of the wire, he also investigated how it elongated under the full range of load, from zero to the breaking point. When he plotted the data for load versus **deformation** on a graph, it formed a near-perfect straight line. This linear relationship between load and deformation is today called Hooke's law, but this groundbreaking discovery was still limited by the fact that Hooke only considered the external forces acting on his specimens. To complete the picture, we need to understand what's happening inside the specimen.

Imagine "cutting" through a **tension member** under load and treating the two halves as separate free bodies. The load is still applied to the end of the lower segment, so the only way it can be in equilibrium is if there's some additional force acting up there on the face of the cut. That is the internal tension force, which must be exactly equal to the external load. The important point is that while internal tension and external load

Galileo's *Two New Sciences* was the world's first comprehensive scientific study of mechanics.

are equal in this setup, they are fundamentally different phenomena. The external load is a concentrated force transmitted to the member or members through a physical connection to another object. The internal force is an attraction between the molecules that constitute this material. The stronger the bond between the molecules, the more they resist being deformed by a load.

In 1822, French mathematician Augustin Cauchy formulated the concept of stress as the internal force divided by the cross-sectional area, expressed in units of force per area. Stress is independent of geometry and material type: When a steel bar with a cross-sectional area of 2 in^2 is loaded with 2000 lbs, the stress on the bar is 2 psi. If a concrete cylinder with a cross-sectional area of 10 in^2 is loaded with 10,000 lbs, the stress is still 1000 psi. Cauchy also defined **strain** as the intensity of deformation, calculated as the amount of deformation divided by the original length of the member. For example, if the member is originally 100 in long and deforms 2 in under load, then the strain is 0.02. Notice that strain has no units; think of it as a percentage.

Today, the results of simple tension tests are recorded as **stress-strain curves**. These are powerful tools because they provide a sort of fingerprint for a material; specimens of different shapes and sizes that are made of the same material should have identical stress-strain curves. The curve tells us almost everything we need to know about a material's mechanical properties and its suitability for a particular structural task.

The linear region of a stress-strain curve has a particularly important characteristic. If we load that specimen within that range and then unload it entirely, the specimen will return to its original length with no permanent deformation. We call this **elastic** behavior. When the stress-strain curve stops being linear—where strain increases but stress is essentially flat—the material is actually stretching like taffy, or yielding, which means the material is beginning to fail. These deformations are permanent; they don't bounce back when the load is removed. We call this **plastic** behavior. With even more strain, the specimen soon fractures.

The three most important properties of an engineering material can be read directly from the stress-strain curve: The curve height corresponds to the largest stress that the material can endure before it fractures—the **ultimate strength** of the material, measured in units of stress. The width of the curve corresponds to the material's capacity to undergo plastic deformations before failure—its **ductility**. The slope of the elastic portion of the curve measures the resistance of the material to nonpermanent deformation—its **stiffness**. Strength is by far the most important of these properties. Engineers need to ensure that the stress on a structure is always less than the strength of the materials, no matter what the externally applied loads are. ■

Important Terms

axial loading: A configuration in which a structural element is subjected only to loads aligned with its longitudinal axis. An axially loaded member must be either in tension or in compression.

cross-section: The geometric shape formed by cutting through a structural element on a plane perpendicular to its length.

cross-sectional area: The area of a cross-section, expressed in units of length squared.

deformation: A change in the shape or dimensions of an object.

ductility: A material's capacity to undergo large, permanent deformations before failing, measured as the strain at fracture or the width of the material's stress-strain curve.

elastic: Material behavior characterized by non-permanent deformations. When a material is behaving elastically, load-induced deformations disappear when the load is removed.

plastic: Material behavior characterized by permanent deformations. When a material is behaving plastically, load-induced deformations remain, even after the load is removed.

stiffness: A material's resistance to elastic deformation, measured as the slope of the lower (elastic) portion of the material's stress-strain curve.

strain: A dimensionless measure of the intensity of deformation.

stress-strain curve: A graph of stress versus strain, used to characterize the engineering properties of a material.

tension member: A structural element that carries load primarily in tension (i.e., by elongating).

ultimate strength: The largest stress a material can withstand before it fractures in tension, measured as the height of the material's stress-strain curve.

yielding: Material behavior characterized by large plastic deformations occurring with little or no increase in load. When a material yields, it begins to fail.

Suggested Reading

Gordon, *Structures*, chap. 2.

Riley, Sturges, and Morris, *Statics and Mechanics of Materials*, chap. 4.

Salvadori, *Why Buildings Stand Up*, chap. 4.

Timoshenko, *History of Strength of Materials*, chap. 1.

Questions to Consider

1. If the stress in a tension member is found to be too large, what 2 ways can the stress be reduced?*

2. If the strain in a tension member is 1.0, how much does it deform?*

3. The stress-strain curves for 3 materials are shown below. Which material is the strongest? Which is stiffest? Which is most ductile?*

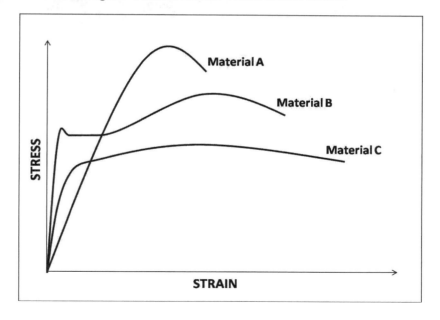

4. Can you identify tension members in this structure—the Marine Way Bridge in the United Kingdom?*

© iStockphoto/Thinkstock.

From Wood to Steel—Properties of Materials
Lecture 4

The difference between the campanile of San Marco and the MetLife Tower can be summarized in one word: steel. The unique properties of steel enabled the MetLife Tower's great height and its efficient use of interior space. This is a typical example of the influence of materials on the form, function, and structure of a great building.

In many respects, steel is an ideal engineering material. Compared to iron, concrete, wood, stone, and brick, steel is superior in all three principal mechanical properties: strength, ductility, and stiffness. The ultimate strength of structural steel is about 65,000 psi, significantly higher than any other materials, and steel has roughly equal strength in tension and compression. Structural steel is very ductile; it can elongate by 25% before fracturing and thus can withstand large plastic deformations and absorb a tremendous amount of energy without failing. Steel is also very stiff; it has a high modulus of elasticity, meaning it takes a lot of stress without elastic deformations. That said, steel has some major limitations: It's susceptible to corrosion and has poor fire resistance.

Wood has been used extensively in building since prehistoric times because of its availability and ease of working. It is the lightest common structural material, about 1/10 the density of steel, but it also has about 1/4 the strength of structural steel; therefore, its strength-to-weight ratio is actually a lot higher than steel's, which, along with its natural beauty, explains why wood is still in use. It has roughly equal strength in tension and compression, which makes it a good material for beams and trusses. However, wood is much less stiff than steel and is relatively brittle. It's subject to rot and is highly flammable. Because it's a natural material, its mechanical properties are much more variable than iron's or steel's. Wood is also subject to creep—long-term increases in deformation, even under consistent load.

Masonry developed in the ancient world in river valley civilizations, where alluvial deposits provided the raw materials for mud bricks. Construction using sun-baked mud brick began at least 10,000 years ago. The frequent maintenance and reconstruction needed at some of the world's largest ancient mud-brick structures illustrate the greatest limitation of mud-brick construction: poor durability. The normal lifespan of a sun-baked mud-brick wall is only about 30 years. Around 3,000 B.C., builders discovered the strength and durability benefits of kiln firing, producing much more durable structures.

Stone masonry also began in prehistoric times, when builders would stack uncut stones and seal the joints with mud mortar. Over time tools and skills improved, and technologies for quarrying and transporting large stones were developed, resulting in structures of unprecedented size and precision, such as the Egyptian pyramids. The pyramids are also our earliest evidence of the systematic technological planning and management we now call engineering.

Both stone and brick masonry have relatively high strength in compression but essentially none in tension, while mortar can't carry any tension; it's there to make masonry watertight and to provide uniform downward transmission of vertical stress. Unlike bricks, large stones can be used as individual structural elements, like beams and columns, and unlike mortar, stone can have substantial tensile strength, though not as much as a metal. Brick and stone were used as load-bearing structural elements well into the 20th century.

Concrete is currently the world's most common construction material. It came into widespread use in the Roman era, around 300 B.C., but was more or less forgotten in the West after the fall of Rome and only returned to common use in the 18th century. Since then, it has been essential for the design and construction of most great structures. Concrete is a combination of 3 basic ingredients: Cement, a fine gray powder; aggregate, a granular material (normally sand and gravel) that gives concrete most of its strength; and water. The water and cement form a paste that hardens in the spaces between the bits of aggregate, effectively creating man-made stone. Roman cement was a mixture of lime and a volcanic ash, and they constructed the inner and outer surfaces of a wall with bricks, then filled the space between with concrete. Modern concrete uses Portland cement, a man-made product, and molds cement into the required shapes.

Concrete fails at a mere 500 psi of tension, so the stress-strain curve for concrete is based on compression. Even in compression, concrete is weaker than steel, but it is cheaper, so engineers use members large cross-sectional areas to get higher compressive strength. Concrete has great fire resistance and reasonably good weather resistance but is quite brittle. Today, this limitation is offset by steel reinforcement, which gives concrete 10 times greater strength in flexure and 50 times greater ductility. Concrete's greatest advantage is its versatility of form.

Steel reinforcement ... gives concrete 10 times greater strength in flexure and 50 times greater ductility.

Structural iron comes in 2 forms: wrought iron, made by smelting (heating and compressing ore to remove impurities and increase ductility); and cast iron (liquefied ore poured into molds). Iron has been produced by human civilizations for roughly 4000 years. Wrought iron dates to Mesopotamia in the 2nd millennium B.C. but was not used for large members until the 2nd century A.D., when the Chinese used it for suspension bridge chains. Cast iron was probably developed in China in the 6th century B.C., but it didn't appear in Europe until about the 14th century. In the 14th and 15th centuries, European iron-making technology advanced in response to military demands. The world's first all-iron structure, the iron bridge at Coalbrookdale, England, was produced in 1779.

Wrought iron has essentially the same properties as steel: strong (but not quite as strong as steel), stiff, and ductile. Cast iron, on the other hand, is brittle and relatively weak in tension. Therefore, we often see 19th-century structures made with cast iron compression members and wrought iron tension members. Iron reigned supreme as a structural material until 1856, when the Bessemer Process made the mass production of high-quality steel possible.

Today, steel is the material of choice for the world's longest bridges and tallest buildings, but its dominance is now being challenged by high-strength concrete. In 1998, the concrete Petronas Towers in Kuala Lumpur, Malaysia, surpassed the steel Sears Tower in Chicago to become the world's tallest building; yet it still depends heavily on steel reinforcement for its load-carrying capacity. ■

Important Terms

aggregate: Granular material (normally sand and gravel) used in concrete.

brittleness: Lack of ductility; the tendency of a material to fail suddenly and catastrophically, without plastic deformation.

cast iron: A construction material made by heating iron to the melting point and then pouring the liquid metal into a mold.

concrete: A material composed of a mixture of cement, water, and aggregate, which hardens into a strong, rock-like mass.

corrosion: Long-term deterioration of iron or steel caused by a chemical reaction with oxygen.

creep: The tendency of a material to experience long-term increases in deformation, even under a constant level of stress.

modulus of elasticity: A material property corresponding to the slope of the elastic portion of a stress-strain curve. It is a measure of the stiffness of a material.

opus latericium: An ancient Roman building system in which concrete was placed between two brick outer walls.

pozzolana: A volcanic ash used as cement in ancient Roman concrete.

steel: A mixture of iron and carbon plus smaller amounts of other elements, such as manganese and chromium.

wrought iron: A construction material made by heating iron ore in a furnace and then beating it with a hammer or flattening it with heavy rollers to remove impurities and increase its ductility.

Suggested Reading

Addis, Building: *3000 Years of Design Engineering and Construction*, chaps. 5–7.

Drysdale, Hamid, and Baker, *Masonry Structures: Behavior and Design*, chap. 1.

Humphrey, Oleson, and Sherwood, *Greek and Roman Technology: A Source book*, pages 243–245 (Roman concrete).

Nilson, Darwin, and Dolan, *Design of Concrete Structures*, chap. 2.

Salvadori, *Why Buildings Stand Up: The Strength of Architecture*, chap. 4.

Sass, *The Substance of Civilization: Materials and Human History from the Stone Age to the Age of Silicon.*

Questions to Consider

1. Why is wood still used as the principal material for residential construction in the U.S.?*

2. Why do you think concrete is the world's most commonly used construction material?*

3. What are some similarities between concrete and cast iron?*

4. Many new engineering materials (e.g., aluminum alloys, plastics, ceramics, fiber-reinforced composites) have been developed since the advent of mass-produced steel in the mid-1800s; yet none of these materials have found widespread use in structures. Why not?*

Building Up—Columns and Buckling
Lecture 5

The two great aspirations of structural engineering are to attain great height and to span long distances. This inherent human inclination to build upward can be seen in the column, ... structural members that carry load primarily in compression, and they've been integral components of the great structures from antiquity all the way to the present day.

The **column** is the most prominent feature of many ancient structures, from Egyptian religious complexes at Karnak to the familiar temples of Classical Greece. Indeed, the Classical Greek architectural orders—Doric, Ionic, and Corinthian—are defined largely in terms of their columns. With the advent of mass-produced iron at the start of the Industrial Revolution, builders began substituting iron for stone, and the first type of structural element to undergo this substitution was the column. Since cast iron is weak in tension but strong in compression, and since columns carry

The column is the signature feature of ancient Greek structures, such as the Parthenon.

loads primarily in compression, this makes perfect sense. Interestingly, the earliest iron columns, while more slender than their stone equivalents, often retained the old Greek shapes and detailing.

Over time, column configurations became more appropriate to the properties of iron, especially in industrial settings, where cost savings trumped aesthetics. This budget consciousness drove efforts to develop optimized iron shapes, such as the I-beam, or I-shaped section. In more recent years, engineers have developed custom-fabricated steel box columns to meet the unique structural demands of tall buildings.

We normally think of columns as being oriented vertically, but in practice, any structural member that carries load primarily in compression exhibits the same behavior independent of its orientation—vertical, horizontal, or diagonal. To avoid confusion, engineers sometimes refer to columns generically as compression members.

The principal load acting on a compression member is its own weight, so the maximum internal force always equals weight. The column's stress is weight over area, but since weight is simply height by density by area, the areas cancel each other out, and we discover that a compression member's stress is its height times its density:

$$\text{stress} = \text{weight/area} = (\text{area} \times \text{height} \times \text{density})/\text{area} = \text{height} \times \text{density}$$

To evaluate the structural performance of a compression member, we use a measure called the **factor of safety**: strength divided by stress must be greater than 1. The larger the factor of safety, the higher the safety margin built into the structure. Look at the 2nd century A.D. Roman monument called Trajan's Column, for example. This 112-ft-tall column is made of marble with a density of 160 lbs/ft^3, which gives us a stress of 124 psi. The strength of marble is about 6000 psi. So the factor of safety is 6000/124, which works out to be 48. Trajan's Column is 48 times stronger than it really needs to be; no wonder it has stood for nearly 2000 years.

When a member's factor of safety is equal to 1 (i.e., stress and strength are equal), that load is called the material failure load. Engineers calculate this as the failure force, which is equal to strength times area.

Another potential failure mode for a compression member is **buckling**. Buckling occurs when a member is subjected to a gradually increasing axial compressive load that causes the member to deflect laterally, often catastrophically. We owe our understanding of buckling to the great Swiss mathematician Leonhard Euler, who developed a mathematical model to predict the axial force at which a member will buckle ($P_{critical}$). The Euler buckling equation is pi squared times the modulus of elasticity (E; i.e., the material's stiffness) times the **area moment of inertia** (I; i.e., the cross-section's resistance to bending, calculated from standard formulas), divided by the column's length (L) squared:

$$P_{critical} = \pi^2 E I / L^2$$

Material has a huge effect on buckling. For example, if you make a column that is 3 ft long and $3/8^2$ in cross-section out of steel, it has a 364-lb buckling load, but if you make it out of wood, it has a 20-lb buckling load. Note, however, that it's not steel's strength in compression that makes the difference, even in a compression member; it's steel's stiffness.

Cross-sectional shape's effect on buckling strength can be predicted by the way the shape distributes material around the member's axis. The further the material is distributed from the axis, the stronger the shape. Daniel Badger's Watervliet Arsenal takes advantage of this fact by using cruciform beams and hollow tubes as compression members.

Length affects buckling strength negatively; that is, the longer the column, the lower its buckling strength (all other factors being equal). Length falls in the denominator of Euler's equation—a large number there would significantly reduce the buckling strength, and length has all the more impact on the calculation because it is squared. Badger offset the effects of length on buckling in the Watervliet Arsenal through lateral bracing, which changes the **effective length** of a column. In general, the strength of a column is determined by the length between points of lateral support, which can be considerably shorter than the overall length of the column.

When comparing a member's buckling strength versus its material failure strength, buckling is what actually controls the maximum possible length for a column. Once a column is short enough that its buckling failure load is less than its material failure load, you don't get any additional advantage against buckling by making it shorter because the material failure load doesn't depend on the length of the member.

In summary, Euler's equation tells us that we can increase the buckling strength of a column in 3 ways: by using a stiffer material, like steel; by using a cross-section with a larger moment of inertia, like a hollow tube; or by keeping the length relatively short. Of these three, length has the greatest influence. ■

Important Terms

area moment of inertia: A measure of a cross-section's resistance to bending.

buckling: A failure mode in which a member in compression suddenly deflects laterally and becomes unstable.

capital: The decorative head on the top of a column.

column: A structural element that carries load primarily in compression; also called a compression member.

effective length: The length of a compression member, measured between points of lateral support.

entasis: A slight outward bulge in the middle of a classical column.

factor of safety: A nondimensional measure of the safety of a structural element, calculated by dividing the failure stress (i.e., the strength) by the actual stress.

Suggested Reading

Gordon, *Structures*, chap. 13.

Riley, Sturges, and Morris. *Statics and Mechanics of Materials*, chap. 11.

Salvadori, *Why Buildings Stand Up*, chap. 5.

Timoshenko, *History of Strength of Materials*, chap. 2.

Questions to Consider

1. An engineer designs two steel structural members—one that carries 10,000 pounds in tension and one that carries 10,000 pounds in compression. Which of the two is likely to be heavier?*

2. If Trajan's Column had been made of iron, rather than stone, what would be the stress at its base? Use 112 ft as the height of the column and 450 lb/ft^3 as the density of iron. If the compressive strength of cast iron is 80,000 psi, what is the factor of safety of this hypothetical iron column?*

3. A steel column has a solid circular cross-section with a 10-inch diameter. Using a calculator or spreadsheet, try plotting a graph of strength versus length for this column, accounting for both material failure and buckling The moment of inertia of a solid circular shape is given by $I = (\pi/4) r^4$, where r is the radius. Use 50,000 psi as the strength of steel and 29,000,000 psi as the modulus of elasticity.*

Building Across—Beams and Bending
Lecture 6

At the heart of the Lion Gate is a stone beam that spans the entire 10-ft opening. This structural element supports its own weight plus the weight of that lion sculpture above it, a total of 30 tons. It's no wonder that later Greeks were awed by this structural achievement. But by the fourth century B.C., descendents of those Greeks who were so awed by Mycenaean construction were building far more impressive structures themselves.

The **beam** combines tension and compression within the same structural member. It is the simplest element that can span a horizontal distance, so it's hardly surprising that we find beams in some of the most ancient structures on earth. Pliny the Elder described the Temple of Artemis at Ephesus as having stone **architrave** beams over 28 ft long and weighing 26 tons. Is that even possible, or is Pliny exaggerating? Once you know a bit more about beams, we'll answer this by using modern scientific principles.

A beam is a structural element that's subjected to transverse loading—that is, loading applied perpendicular to the member's axis. It responds to the transverse load by bending. In engineering mechanics, this is called **flexure**, and it has two fundamental characteristics: First, one side of the beam experiences compression and the other side experiences tension. Second, this combination of tension and compression causes the beam to deform into a curve.

Like a column, a beam has three main physical characteristics: its support configuration, its cross-section, and its **profile**. The most common support configurations are simple, cantilever, and continuous. Each end of a **simply supported beam** rests on a single support and under load bends into single curvature with the concave surface upward. A **cantilever beam** is fixed at one end and unsupported at the other; when loaded, it bends so that the concave side faces downward. A **continuous beam** has a fixed support at each end and at one or more points along its length. A continuous beam with one intermediate support shows concave-up flexure at each end and concave-down flexure at the center support. Because of that change in direction of the curvature, continuous beams can be significantly more structurally efficient than simply supported beams.

Many beams have rectangular cross sections, although most modern steel beams have I-shaped cross-sections. Many reinforced concrete beams are I-shaped as well, although some are hollow boxes. On any I-shaped member, the horizontal plates are called **flanges** and the vertical one is called the **web**.

The profile of a beam is its shape when viewed from the side. Most beams, from ancient times to today, are rectangular in profile, but they may be curved as well—thicker on the ends and thinner in the middle or vice versa.

Let's examine beams in action, using those huge architrave beams of the ancient Temple of Artemis in Ephesus. For this beam, the principal load is its own weight. This is a **distributed load**, meaning it is spread uniformly along the entire length of the member, in this case at 1860 lbs/ft. The principle of equilibrium tells us that this 52,000-lb downward load causes two 26,000-lb reactions, one at each end. The compression of the beam's concave side and the tension on its convex side must also be in equilibrium, because they're the only horizontal forces working on the beam. The combined compression and tension cause rotation—an **internal moment**—within the beam. Internal moment varies along the length of the member at any given point, but along the member as a whole it forms a perfect parabolic curve.

In 1826, a French engineer and physicist named Claude-Louis Navier formulated and published the scientific principles of flexure that we still use today. Navier not only observed that when a beam bends, we get compression on one side and tension on the other but more specifically that between those extremes is a linear gradient of stress. Based on these insights, Navier formulated a complete mathematical model manifested in a single equation for calculating the maximum stress in any beam, for any loading condition. In brief, the equation shows that stress in a beam increases with internal moment and decreases with the area moment of inertia. Applying Navier's equation to the Temple of Artemis architrave beams, we get an estimated maximum stress of 200 psi, whereas 1,000 psi is a reasonable estimate for marble. Based on this analysis, there is no reason to doubt Pliny's account of the size of the beams.

Why do so many modern beams use I-shaped and hollow box cross-sections, rather than rectangular? It turns out that I-shaped beams have significantly greater resistance to bending because more material is located farther away from the axis; they have a larger area moment of inertia and thus, according to Navier's equation, lower stress. However, I-shaped beams are particularly susceptible to torsion, or twisting. A hollow box section is quite strong in torsion because it has a closed shape, and it has a large moment of inertia compared with an equivalent rectangular section.

> **The combined compression and tension cause rotation—an internal moment—within the beam.**

What about the varying profiles and support configurations we find in beams? Navier's equation tells us that higher internal moment causes higher stress, while a larger moment of inertia reduces stress. We can increase a beam's moment of inertia by making it deeper; a truly optimal beam design could be achieved by making the profile of the beam match the parabolic curve of its moment diagram. The deep portions of the beam provide greater resistance to bending at precisely the locations where that greater resistance is required. In the Raftsundet Bridge, we see the ultimate product of science-based engineering: a beam with supports and profile that are matched to the moment diagram and a cross-section that achieves optimal resistance to both bending and torsion; in short, a structure that's perfectly tuned to its load-carrying purpose. ■

Important Terms

architrave: A horizontal stone beam spanning across the tops of the columns in a classical portico.

beam: A structural element that is subjected to transverse loading and carries load in bending.

box girder: A beam with a hollow rectangular or trapezoidal cross-section.

cantilever beam: A beam supported at one end and unsupported at the other. The single support must prevent the supported end of the beam from rotating.

continuous beam: A beam supported at each end and extending continuously across one or more intermediate supports.

distributed load: A load that is spread uniformly along the length of the member. A distributed load is expressed in units of force per length.

flange: Horizontal element of an I-shaped cross-section.

flexure: The structural behavior of a beam, characterized by the deformation of the member into a curved shape, with compression occurring on the concave side and tension occurring on the convex side.

internal moment: A moment caused by the internal tension and compression forces in a beam.

moment diagram: A graph of internal moment versus length.

plate girder: An I-shaped beam constructed by riveting or welding individual plates or angles together.

portico: A covered porch at the entrance of a building.

profile: The shape of a structural element when viewed from the side.

simply supported beam: A beam with one support at each end. These supports provide no resistance to rotation.

web: The vertical element of an I-shaped cross-section.

Gordon, *Structures*, chap. 11.

Riley, Sturges, and Morris. *Statics and Mechanics of Materials*, chap. 8.

Salvadori, *Why Buildings Stand Up*, chap. 5.

Timoshenko, *History of Strength of Materials*, chaps. 1 and 4.

Questions to Consider

1. Where would you expect to find the maximum internal moment in the two beams below?

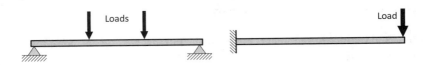

2. If the stress in a beam is found to be too large, how can the stress be reduced?*

3. If a continuous beam is more efficient than a simply supported beam, why are so many simply supported beams used in modern structures?*

4. Sketch the deflected shape of a two-span continuous beam, subject to a single concentrated load as shown below. Where does the beam bend concave upward? Where does it bend concave downward? Where will tension occur? Where will compression occur? Can you guess the approximate shape of the moment diagram for this beam?*

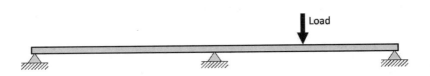

Lecture 6: Building Across—Beams and Bending

Trusses—The Power of the Triangle
Lecture 7

From a distance we admire the tower's graceful form, but as we get closer we can see that this entire structure is actually composed of a network of members arranged in interconnected triangles. The Eiffel Tower is, therefore, a truss. ... As we zoom in even closer, we can see that most of the individual structural elements ... are built up of iron bars arranged in interconnected triangles. These individual members of the Eiffel Tower are trusses within a truss.

A **truss** is a rigid framework composed of members connected at joints and arranged into a network of triangles. The triangle is an inherently stable structural configuration, and it's the principal source of a truss's structural rigidity. Trusses are inherently strong, stiff, and light. They can span long distances or reach great heights with many small elements, rather than a few large ones. Also, trusses allow for great versatility of form, enabling the construction of graceful curves out of straight structural members.

First, some terminology: The members that run the outer length of a truss structure are called the top and bottom **chords**. Those that connect the chords are called **verticals** or **diagonals**, depending on

Gustave Eiffel's landmark tower is a series of trusses, meticulously arranged into graceful curves.

their orientation. Truss members come in various shapes, from cruciform and T-shapes to slender circular rods. The shape used is dictated by the structural needs of the body.

The use of trusses has varied considerably through the ages. It was developed in antiquity, though we don't know precisely when; the ancient Greeks did not use them, but the Romans did, although they occasionally used quadrilateral trusses. Early Christian churches adopted the Roman basilica form, including its roof-trussing system; 700 years later, a similar roof system was still being used in medieval churches, with one important difference: medieval architects used all triangle trusses. All of these early trusses were made of wood and have heavy, stocky proportions—a good indicator that they were designed empirically, with no structural optimization. The second generation in truss design arrived with the advent of mass-produced iron in the 19th century. Among the earliest uses of iron trusses was this roof over the passenger platform at London's Euston Station, constructed in 1838. The geometry of these trusses is nearly identical to medieval wooden roof trusses, yet the members are slender. The unique properties of iron were driving structural innovations.

An American engineer named Squire Whipple developed the iron bowstring truss and patented it in 1841. It was almost certainly the first scientifically designed truss in the United States, probably in the world. In 1847, Whipple's *A Work on Bridge Building* described, for the first time ever, a fully rational, science-based process for analyzing and designing trusses, and his "method of joints" is still taught and used in engineering today. In brief, the method calculates the internal forces in every member of a truss structure by using a graphical concept called the **polygon of forces**. The forces acting on a body in equilibrium can be drawn as a closed polygon where the angles are the same as the real-world body's angles, but the length of each side is proportional to the magnitude of the internal force acting on it. The equation behind any polygon of forces will require some trigonometry because it deals with angles as well as lines, but otherwise, it's the same as any other equilibrium problem. You're just balancing forces.

When you calculate all of the internal member forces in a truss, you'll find all the top chord members are in compression and all the bottom chord members are in tension. In fact, a truss behaves exactly like a beam when it's subjected to transverse loading: It bends, compressing the top surface and tensioning the bottom surface. Some of the diagonals of the truss will be in compression and others in tension, but the tension in the diagonals will be quite a bit less than the tension in the bottom chord members. You'll also find that your calculated results are pretty predictable simply by looking at the members of the body itself; their shapes and proportions will communicate how it carries its load.

Whipple's *A Work on Bridge Building* described, for the first time ever, a fully rational, science-based process for analyzing and designing trusses.

We can also learn a lot about a truss by examining its structural connections. Single-bolt connections were common in the 19th century because Whipple's equations—for simplicity's sake—assume a single, frictionless pin at each joint. Rather than the mathematical model mimicking reality, reality was mimicking the mathematical model. Today, single-bolt connections are considered poor engineering because there's no redundancy if the bolt should fail.

In the century following Whipple's publication of *A Work on Bridge Building*, trusses were incorporated into many of the world's great structures. Because engineers could now predict their designs' behavior with greater confidence, they were emboldened to design larger and more sophisticated trusses and use them in exciting new ways: in long-span roofs, in magnificent arched bridges, in the Brooklyn Bridge and most of the great suspension bridges of that era, and in cantilever bridges. They also moved away from Whipple's simple pinned connections to the more complex but safer gusset plate connection, made from steel plates joined with multiple rivets or bolts.

Today, trusses aren't quite as common in great structures. Today, labor costs are much higher relative to materials. Trusses are labor-intensive structures, and labor costs are much higher today than in the 19th century. Trusses are more often used on projects that can take advantage of the cost savings of mass production—highway sign supports, cell phone towers, and the like. Yet trusses can still be used to glorious aesthetic effect, as in I. M. Pei's famous steel and glass pyramid, the main entrance to the Louvre Museum. The inner structure of these sloped walls is an elaborate 3-dimensional truss—light, strong, and geometrically fascinating. ■

Important Terms

chord: A structural member that extends along the top or bottom of a truss.

diagonal: A diagonally oriented truss member.

polygon of forces: A graphical method of applying the principle of equilibrium. If a system of forces is in equilibrium, then those forces, drawn to scale, will form a closed polygon.

truss: A structure consisting of elements arranged in interconnected triangles. These elements carry load primarily in tension or compression.

vertical: A vertically oriented truss member.

Suggested Reading

Addis, *Building*, chap. 6.

Riley, Sturges, and Morris. *Statics and Mechanics of Materials*, chap. 6.

Salvadori, *Why Buildings Stand Up*, chap. 8.

Timoshenko, *History of Strength of Materials*, p. 181–97.

Questions to Consider

1. Nearly all trusses are made of wood or metal. Why are trusses generally not made of stone or concrete?*

2. The railroad bridge below consists of 2 main trusses, connected together with transverse members and diagonal braces. Draw a free body diagram of *one* main truss, assuming that the only load is a 100,000-pound locomotive at mid-span. For simplicity, we will assume that this load is

applied as a single concentrated load at the center bottom-chord joint. We will also assume that the self-weight of the truss is negligible, in comparison with the weight of the locomotive. The span of this bridge is 100 ft, and its height is 40 ft.*

Library of Congress, Prints and Photographs Division.

3. For the truss you sketched in Question 2, use the Method of Joints to calculate the internal forces in the top and bottom chords.*

4. Based solely on their proportions, which structural elements of this truss do you expect to be in compression? In tension?*

5. Based on the connections used in this bridge, can you estimate its age?*

Cables and Arches—The Power of the Parabola
Lecture 8

When you look at the majestic curve of the Saint Louis Gateway Arch and the graceful sweep of the main cables of the Golden Gate Bridge, has it ever occurred to you that their principal structural elements— the cable and the arch—have exactly the same shape? If so, did you ever wonder if there's an underlying scientific reason why the designers of these structures chose the same shape?

Cables come in 2 basic configurations—cables supporting a uniform load distributed all along their length and cables supporting a horizontally distributed load suspended below them. Cables of the first type suspended from 2 points of equal height naturally fall into a curved shape called a **catenary**. The distance between the supports is the span of a cable; this is different from the length of the cable, which is the amount of cable needed to drape between the 2 supports and is always at least a little greater than the span. The vertical distance from the point of support to the lowest point of the cable's curve is the sag. The only load acting on the cable is its own weight, which is uniformly distributed along the length. It carries its load entirely in tension; after all, you can't push a rope. This form of cable structure was used in suspension bridges in China as early as the 3rd century B.C. For the second type of cable, the load consists of a series of equal weights equally spaced along a horizontal plane below the cable. The weight of the cable itself is negligible compared with the load hanging from it. This configuration is more representative of a modern suspension bridge.

The internal tension on a cable is expressed as 3 equations. First, the horizontal reaction (H) is equal to the cable tension (T); so the greater the tension, the greater the outward pull needed to hold the cable in place. Second, the vertical reaction is equal to half of the load applied to the cable. In a suspension bridge, the cable transmits this same force downward into the towers. Thus, the greater the load and the longer the span, the greater the downward force applied to the towers. Third, the cable tension is proportional to the load and inversely proportional to the sag. So if we hold the sag constant, a larger load causes larger cable tension. If we hold the load constant, then a larger tension results in less cable sag.

An equilibrium analysis performed at exactly mid-span indicates that the curve of the cable is a catenary; however, measured elsewhere, the shape of the cable with a horizontally distributed load suspended beneath seems to be a **parabola**. This brings us to a unique aspect of cable behavior: The shape of a cable always depends on its loading. In other words, a cable assumes whatever shape is necessary to maintain equilibrium. The difference between a parabola and a catenary is extremely small, and furthermore, in practice no suspension bridge cable is a perfect parabola or a perfect catenary because it carries both its own weight (which causes it to tend toward the catenary) and the weight of the deck (which tends toward the shape of a parabola).

In many ways, an **arch** is the exact opposite of a cable. One of its fundamental characteristics is that it isn't self-supporting until it's finished. When the Romans built an arch, they began with a temporary support structure called a **centering**, then added the wedge-shaped stones called **voussoirs** up each

The St. Louis Gateway Arch and the nearby Eads Bridge, although they serve different purposes, share a common shape.

side until they could place the final keystone. Once the keystone is in place, an arch is capable of carrying its own load plus significant compression force as well.

This arch has two essential structural characteristics: First, it carries load entirely in compression, as demonstrated by the lack of any mortar or adhesive holding the voussoirs together. If you apply tension to an arch, the blocks simply fall apart. This characteristic accounts for the use of arches in many of the ancient world's greatest structures; the basic materials available to them, such as stone, brick, and concrete, were strong in compression but weak in tension. An arch made of these materials can support a far greater load than a beam of the same length, which would have to take some tension. Arches can be made of lower-quality materials because even large flaws don't reduce a member's ability to carry compression.

The second characteristic of an arch is that it requires both vertical and horizontal reactions to carry load. The downward load of the arch is balanced by an upward reaction from the base, but an engineer needs to integrate inward horizontal reactions into any arch design, or the arch will tend to flatten outward. This outward tendency is called **thrust**. When we solve the equilibrium equations, we get exactly the same horizontal force results we got for the cable, except now they're compression rather than tension. It's worth remembering that the horizontal thrust of an arch is inversely proportional to its height; a taller arch produces less thrust than a flatter arch.

In the 1600s, Robert Hooke calculated that if the arch supports only its own weight, its ideal shape is a catenary, and if it supports a horizontally distributed load, its ideal shape is a parabola. So why are all Roman arches semicircular, and how did they survive? The Romans, although great builders, could only work from experience, not science. Through trial (and no doubt error) the Romans learned that as long as the **thrust line** of an arch—the path of its internal compression—remains entirely within the arch's boundaries, the arch remains stable. Roman semicircular arches are thick enough to completely contain their parabolic thrust lines.

So to summarize, a cable carries load entirely in tension; an arch carries load entirely in compression. Tension on a cable pulls inward on its supports; and thrust from an arch pushes outward. A cable and an arch both require both vertical and horizontal reactions to carry load, and the horizontal reactions are inversely proportional to the height. They have the same optimal shapes under similar loading conditions: catenary and parabola. In a sense, they are 2 sides of the same coin. ■

Important Terms

arch: A structural element that, because of its shape and support configuration, carries load primarily in compression.

cable: A flexible structural element that carries load entirely in tension and changes its shape in response to the applied loading.

catenary: The curved shape of a draped cable subjected to a uniform loading distributed along the cable's length.

centering: A temporary structure used to support an arch while it is being constructed.

jack arch: A flat arch.

parabola: The curved shape of a draped cable subjected to a uniform horizontally distributed loading.

thrust: The outward force exerted by an arch on its supports, caused by the tendency of an arch to spread outward under load.

thrust line: A graphical representation of the path of the internal compression force through a structural element.

voussoir: A wedge-shaped element of an arch.

Addis, *Building*, chap. 4.

Salvadori, *Why Buildings Stand Up*, chap. 9.

Timoshenko, *History of Strength of Materials*, p. 62–6.

Questions to Consider

1. Each main cable of the Golden Gate Bridge spans 4200 ft between the two towers. The cable sag is 500 ft. For a total load (dead load plus traffic load) of 20,000 pounds per foot, what is the internal force in one cable at mid-span?*

2. The simple structure below is composed of 2 members connected with pinned joints. Although it might not look like one, this structure is an arch. Can you explain why?*

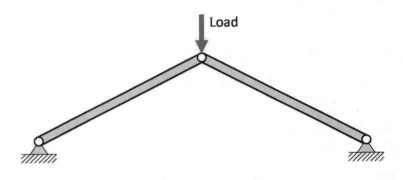

3. The photo below shows two arch bridges—a lower bridge in the foreground that spans the river with a single shallow arch and taller bridge in the background that uses a series of shorter, deeper arches. Why might the design engineers have used these two different configurations at the same site?*

© iStockphoto/Thinkstock.

Loads and Structural Systems
Lecture 9

Trajan's Column is just a column; and unlike most columns, it supports no other structural elements. ... The St. Louis Gateway Arch is just an arch, at least when viewed from the outside; but on the inside, there's actually a fairly complex structural system that's used to support the tram. ... So maybe it isn't "just an arch" after all; and that's the point: Standalone structural elements are rare.

In the real world, very few structural elements stand alone, with their own external loads and reactions. Most are components of structural systems—assemblies of multiple interconnected load-carrying elements. To analyze a structural system, you must analyze not only the individual elements but how those elements transmit forces through the entire body. We call this chain of elements and connections a load path.

To analyze the load path of the church of San Miniato al Monte in Florence, Italy, we begin with the roof, which is the principal load on the building. The roof is supported by longitudinal beams, which carry load in flexure and transmit loads to a series of trusses just below. Both beams and trusses generate vertical reactions at each end, down into the walls. There's also a back wall that is peaked and follows the same alignment as the roof trusses. It carries part of the roof load vertically, but it also stabilizes the side walls horizontally. San Miniato al Monte has a central nave and 2 side aisles. The bottoms of the nave walls are a series of arches that open into the aisles. Finally, there are 6 principal structural columns. At each stage in this load path, each element carries not just its own weight but the weight of every other element above it in the path. By that logic, you see that the columns are carrying the entire weight of the building and transmitting it into the foundations via direct axial compression.

Structural systems are heavily influenced by the loads they're designed to carry, both the dead load of the structure itself and the live load of a changing environment. Wind and earthquake loads dominate the design of skyscrapers; snow load dominates the design of flat-roofed buildings in northern climates. The most important live loads are traffic loads, occupancy loads, and environmental loads due to wind, snow, and earthquakes. All structures must be designed to resist all relevant loads, and each type of load may have its own distinct load path.

Dead loads are estimated at the beginning of the design process and checked and updated later once the sizes of all the structural members have actually been determined. This process usually requires a couple of iterations because each update of the dead loads can change the required sizes of the members, which, of course, changes the dead load again. As tedious as this seems, this process is fundamental to structural design; if done improperly, catastrophe can result.

Designing for **traffic loads**—the weight of cars, trucks, trains, and anything else crossing a bridge—is challenging because the loading may change so much over time from traffic volume, traffic type, and even road resurfacing. **Occupancy loads**—the weight of people, furniture, and movable equipment in buildings—are similarly hard to calculate because they vary so much over the lifetime of the structure. To calculate **wind loads**, you have to take into account not just pressure on the windward face but a vacuum created on the leeward side by the circulation of air around the structure. **Snow load**, for obvious reasons, has the most influence on structural design in cold, wet climates. In some regions,

The Romans, without a mathematical understanding of mechanics, made Trajan's Column several times stronger than it needed to be.

49

snow load can be as high as 100 lb/ft² of roof surface; at that intensity, even a modest single-family home would have to be designed for upwards of 150,000 lbs of snow on its roof.

Unlike other loads, an **earthquake load** is not a force but an acceleration. In an earthquake, the ground moves rapidly, and mostly horizontally, beneath a structure. At first the building tries to stand still, but once the ground has moved some distance, the building has to follow. **Newton's second law** tells us that force is equal to mass times acceleration; thus the mass of the building being accelerated laterally is equivalent to a force. That's why engineers represent the lateral motion of a building in an earthquake as a lateral force.

Thus far, we've seen 2 of Newton's 3 laws of motion in practice in engineering design. **Newton's third law** says that for every action, there is an equal and opposite reaction. This might sound similar to the principle of equilibrium, but it applies more specifically to the point of contact between the bodies, the actual location where the equal and opposite forces meet. When analyzing load paths, it's important to remember that force is transmitted through these specific points of jointure. It also enables us to conceptually "flip" upward reactions in a structure and think of them as downward loads on supporting structural elements.

As you can see, the load path is not some vague or theoretical concept; it's a real, physical pathway that we can visually trace through the structure from top to bottom. Now that you understand the mechanics of our 6 basic structural elements and how they transmit load through an entire body, it's time to look at these principles in the real world of great structures. ■

Important Terms

earthquake load: The effect of earthquake-induced ground motion on a structure.

Newton's second law: An unbalanced force acting on a body causes the body to accelerate. The relationship between the force (F) and the acceleration (a) is given by the equation $F = ma$, where m is the mass of the body.

Newton's third law: For every action, there is an equal and opposite reaction.

occupancy load: The weight of people, furniture, and movable equipment in a building.

snow load: The weight of snow accumulating on a roof, bridge deck, or other surface.

traffic load: The weight of cars, trucks, trains, and other vehicles crossing a bridge.

wind load: The pressure exerted by wind striking and flowing around a structure.

Suggested Reading

American Society of Civil Engineers, *Minimum Design Loads for Buildings and Other Structures*, chaps. 3, 4, 6, 7, and 9.

Questions to Consider

1. Estimate the largest possible occupancy load (in pounds) that could be applied to your kitchen floor. (Hint: Determine the largest possible number of people that could fit into the room; then multiply this number by an estimated average weight per person).

2. Should a bridge be designed to carry the maximum possible snow load and the maximum possible traffic load simultaneously?*

3. Explain how the garden swing, pictured below, works as a structural system. (Be sure to consider *all elements* in the load path, starting where the load is applied and ending at the structural foundation.)*

© iStockphoto/Thinkstock.

Egypt and Greece—Pyramids to the Parthenon
Lecture 10

The pyramids: They're important, not just because they're great structures, but also because they represent some of the earliest human achievements that can legitimately be called "engineering."

Now we begin to put your new knowledge of structural elements and structural systems to use with in-depth examinations of great structures. In doing so, we'll be drawing on 4 big ideas: the basic scientific principles of engineering mechanics, which provide the tools that we need to understand how structural elements carry load; the concept of a structural system as we talked about last lecture, which allows us to understand the interactions between structural elements; the highly variable relationship between form, function, and structure; and finally, the notion that understanding structure depends not only on physical characteristics but also on historical context.

Egypt's pyramids are important not just because they're great structures but also because they are some of the earliest human achievements that can legitimately be called engineering. Heavy stone masonry required expertise for quarrying and moving stones; estimating construction time and material quantities; surveying a site; and organizing a large workforce. The Great Pyramid of Giza, built in the 26th century B.C., was constructed from over 2 million limestone blocks weighing 2 tons each. Its interior granite was transported from more than 500 miles away, and the project was finished in just 20 years. It was the tallest structure on earth until the 14th century A.D. All this was accomplished before the invention of the wheel, the pulley, or iron tools.

Structurally, the pyramids are simple: man-made mountains carrying their own weight through internal compression. Yet inside they reflect some surprisingly adept structural engineering. The roof slab of the King's Chamber in the Great Pyramid is capable of carrying 60 times greater stress than its own tensile stress. The 5 empty chambers above it are topped with a primitive, pointed, relieving arch, so that none of the millions of tons of stone above puts stress on the King's Chamber.

The Meidum Pyramid was a step pyramid constructed by Pharaoh Huni around 2630 B.C. Huni's successor converted it into a true pyramid by filling in the steps with a limestone casing; today, that casing lies as rubble around the step pyramid's base—the result of a catastrophic collapse caused by settlement of the soft, sand foundation under the casing and the casing's horizontal masonry configuration. Perhaps as a result of this lesson, the Bent Pyramid and Red Pyramid of Dashur were constructed with walls at a 43.5° angle instead of the standard 52°, reducing their weight and increasing their stability. Subsequently, Egyptian builders only constructed 52° pyramids on foundations of solid bedrock.

Shifting from Egypt to Mycenae, the center of early Greek civilization, we find the Treasury of Atreus, a circular tomb with a **corbelled dome** built

© iStockphoto/Thinkstock.

Although they seem simple from the outside, on the inside the Pyramids of Giza reveal extraordinarily complex engineering.

around 1250 B.C. To understand the corbelled dome, we need to look at its antecedent, the corbelled arch, or false arch. A **corbelled arch** is constructed of horizontal layers (called courses) of stone, with each layer extending a little beyond the layer below. Each projecting stone acts as a cantilevered beam, so unlike a **true arch**, a corbelled arch carries some force in tension. The lower layers actually need the upper layers to stabilize the arch; otherwise, it would fall in on itself. An important advantage of this kind of arch is that it can be constructed without using temporary centering.

A corbelled dome can be visualized as a corbelled arch rotated around its central vertical axis. However, because of the outer slope of the dome, the successive layers of stone do not add stability but tend to tilt inward. Thus, in ancient times, all corbelled domes were built underground, stabilizing the successive layers of masonry with lateral earth pressure. The stone is really only half of the structural system of a corbelled dome; the system couldn't carry load effectively without the earth.

About 50 miles away from Mycenae was the great city-state of Athens. Although influenced by their Egyptian neighbors, the Greeks constructed more modest structures and replicated them all over the region via the first formal system of building design in recorded history. Vitruvius's *De architectura* describes the Greeks' empirical rules for temple design, which define a single dimensional module equal to the radius of a column in the temple portico, then specify all other dimensions of the building in terms of that module. Like a modern mathematical model, this system allowed the designer to try out various alternatives and reliably evaluate the results. These geometric design rules were a seed of modern science-based design.

No structure better exemplifies the Greeks' love of geometry than the Parthenon. Its architects were subordinate to a sculptor, Phidias, so form dominates structure in this building. The roof was a wooden deck covered with marble tiles, supported on longitudinal timber beams, supported on vertical posts, supported on transverse beams. The transverse beams were supported on 3 concentric rings of vertical stone: the outer **colonnade**, the middle walls, and the central colonnade, which only existed to support the roof. Had the Greeks discovered the truss, there would have been no need for inner support, which actually hinders the use of the temple by crowding the **cella** where the goddess's statue is kept. For all of its architectural magnificence, the Parthenon has a rather unsophisticated structural design. ■

Important Terms

cella: The sanctuary of a Greek temple, housing a statue of the god or goddess to whom the temple is dedicated.

collonade: A grouping of columns placed at regular intervals.

corbelled arch: A "false arch" constructed of horizontal layers of stone or brick. A corbelled arch is created by cantilevering successive layers of stone inward from each side of an opening, until they meet in the center.

corbelled dome: A dome built of horizontal layers of stone or brick. Each layer is a circular ring of masonry, and each successive layer is slightly smaller than the one below.

true arch: An arch constructed of wedge-shaped voussoirs, as distinguished from a corbelled arch.

tryglyph: A rectangular architectural feature on the frieze of a Greek temple.

Suggested Reading

Addis, *Building*, chap. 1.

Drysdale, Hamid, and Baker, *Masonry Structures*, chap. 1.

Gordon, *Structures*, chap. 11.

Nuttgens, *The Story of Architecture*, chaps. 1, 2, 3, and 7.

Salvadori, *Why Buildings Stand Up*, chap. 2.

Questions to Consider

1. In what ways do the great structures of Egypt, Mycenae, and Athens reflect their respective civilizations?

2. What is the relationship between form, function, and structure in the Treasury of Atreus?*

3. What are some important differences between the structural behavior of a corbelled arch and that of a true arch?*

4. Why did Greek structural technologies fall out of use with the decline of classical Greek civilization, even though Greek architectural forms are still used today?

The Glory of Rome in Arches and Vaults
Lecture 11

> When I think of Rome, the first image that comes to mind is an arch.
> … It's present in bridges that carried the famous Roman roads to the
> far-flung corners of the empire. It's present in monumental aqueducts
> that brought fresh water to the cities, and in sewers that carried away
> the effluent. It's there in triumphal arches that celebrated the victories
> of the Legions, and in the city gates that kept enemies at bay.

A mong the earliest engineers, the principal technology for spanning long, horizontal distances was the beam; it was the Etruscans, an early Italic people, who introduced the arch and the Romans who used it to open a whole new realm of structural possibility. Because the arch carries load entirely in compression, its span isn't limited by the tensile strength of the material or the size of its individual stones, and it can span greater distances than could even be conceived of with stone beams—but only if it has adequate lateral restraint.

The 1st-century B.C. Pont Saint Martin demonstrates the simplest form of arched structure—a single semicircular arch supporting a single-lane roadway—yet this 103-ft span is among the largest surviving Roman structures. The steep, rocky river valley it crosses provides both vertical and horizontal support, enhanced with masonry. The ledges used to support the arch's temporary wooden centering during construction were engineered right into the structure of the bridge. On top of the arch ring are 2 spandrels— stone walls—the space between them filled with concrete, then topped with pavimentum, the typical Roman road surface. The spandrels also help prevent structural failure by preventing the ends of the span from bulging under concentrated live loads.

The Pons Fabricius, located in the heart of Rome, was built in 62 B.C.—the oldest fully intact Roman bridge in Italy. Its structural system is essentially the same as the Pont Saint Martin's, except that there are now 2 main arches. The inner ends of the arches are supported vertically on the large central pier, and the horizontal thrusts from the arches oppose each other and cancel each other out. Thus in an arcade, a series of arches, the outward thrusts of adjacent arches counteract each other, so interior arch supports don't need to be as substantial as the end supports. To resist the live load of flooding, the central pier is far more massive than it needs to be just to support the arches and contains a channel for water to pass through.

The Pont du Gard, built by the Romans in southern France in the 1st century B.C., is a 3-level arcade that acts as both a bridge and an aqueduct. Constructed of stone, its individual blocks were fitted so closely that no mortar was needed to hold them together. The bases of the interior arches have only vertical reactions because the adjacent arches cancel each other out, but the outermost arches must be laterally supported with substantial foundations built into the riverbanks. The Roman aqueduct at Segovia, Spain, built around A.D. 100, isn't as tall as the Pont du Gard, but it's considerably longer. Its arches rest on tall, slender stone columns, dramatically demonstrating the counterbalance between its interior arches.

In free-standing single arches, like the triumphal Arch of Titus in Rome, the lateral thrust of the arch tends to tip the columns outward slightly, causing the arch to flatten. The outward horizontal thrust is applied at the inside of the arch, so the inward reaction at the base occurs at the outside of each column. In other words, the column is tending to rotate about that corner. Think of the column as being acted on by 2 different moments: an overturning moment (the thrust times the height) and a stabilizing moment caused by the weight of the column itself (its weight times half of the distance). Therefore, to minimize the overturning moment and maximize the

© Photos.com/Thinkstock.

The heavy, squat shape of the Arch of Titus in Rome helps this free-standing arch resist its own tendency to overturn.

stabilizing moment, we can reduce the height of the column, increase its weight, or increase its width. The Arch of Titus has short, wide, heavy piers for just that reason.

Once the arch had proved effective in spanning horizontal distances, it was adapted to enclosing spaces. When an arch is extended to form a roof or ceiling, it's called a barrel vault. The fundamental structure of the Roman Colosseum is a series of 80 barrel vaults arranged radially around the first level, forming the entrances as well as the foundations for the upper arcades and the concrete seating areas. The vaults require no external lateral support because they're arranged in an ellipse; every arch is laterally supported by its neighbors. It is one of the most famous buildings in the Western world, yet in its historical context, the Colosseum was unremarkable—neither a particularly large nor particularly innovative example of a Roman amphitheater.

> **Once the arch had proved effective in spanning horizontal distances, it was adapted to enclosing spaces.**

The 3rd-century A.D. Baths of Caracalla, on the other hand, were a stunning achievement that wouldn't be exceeded in scale until the late medieval period. Perhaps its most impressive feature is the expanse of groined vaulting that forms the ceiling. A groined vault is formed by 2 barrel vaults intersecting at a right angle, subdividing the interior space into square or rectangular bays. The vaults allowed for large window openings high in the walls. Groined vaults were so successful that they was used in Romanesque and Gothic cathedral architecture for the next 1000 years and influence public buildings to this day.

Like any arch or vault, a groined vault produces lateral thrust. Roman engineers reduced thrust in 2 main ways: by casting octagonal coffers into the vaults, reducing their self-weight; and by constructing smaller, perpendicular barrel vaults to buttress the structural system. This innovation would also profoundly affect architecture for centuries to come. ■

Important Terms

aqueduct: A structure that carries a water channel.

arcade: A row of adjacent arches, usually supported on columns.

barrel vault: A curved roof shaped like half of a cylinder, normally supported on two parallel walls.

buttress vault: A barrel vault used to restrain the lateral thrust of a larger vault, arch, or dome.

caldarium: The hot room in a Roman bath.

coffer: A polygonal indentation in a vault, dome, or ceiling.

frigidarium: The cold room in a Roman bath.

groined vault: A vault formed by the intersection of two perpendicular barrel vaults.

pavimentum: A layer of granular material like crushed stone or tile, mixed with lime or cement, used as a road surface in Roman construction.

spandrel: A triangular wall that fills in the space above an arch.

tepidarium: The medium-temperature room in a Roman bath.

Important Terms

Addis, *Building*, chap. 1.

De Camp, *The Ancient Engineers*, chaps. 6–7.

Gordon, *Structures*, chap. 9.

Nuttgens, *The Story of Architecture*, chap. 8.

1. What is the relationship between form, function, and structure in the frigidarium of the Baths of Caracalla?*

2. What methods did Roman engineers use to restrain the lateral thrust of arches and vaults? How did these various techniques influence the form of Roman structures?*

3. The Basilica of Maxentius (A.D. 308–312) was nearly identical to the frigidarium of the Baths of Caracalla (A.D. 212–216) but larger. What does this tell us about how the Romans developed engineering expertise and construction methods?*

4. Can you think of a modern building or bridge that incorporates structural concepts developed by the Romans?*

The Rise and Fall of the Gothic Cathedral
Lecture 12

Saint Pierre in the town of Beauvais: Begun in 1247, it was to be the tallest cathedral in the world; the true pinnacle of Gothic architecture. But in 1284, with only the apse completed, a large portion of the vaulted ceiling collapsed. ... It is a rich case study in the development of Gothic architecture and the limits of empirical design, literally written into the walls of the building.

Arches fell on hard times with the fall of the Western Roman Empire in the 5th century A.D. The imperial stimulus for technological innovation disappeared, and the Roman system for training engineers collapsed. Not until the 11th century were significant numbers of major construction projects undertaken again in Europe, and they were of 2 types: fortifications and churches. From a structural engineering perspective, churches are far more interesting.

In late antiquity and in the early medieval period, Christians adopted the Romans's standard civic building, the basilica, for many of their churches. A basilica is a simple rectangular hall with a semicircular apse at the short end opposite the main entrance. Between the Roman era and the 11th century, the only substantial change to the basilica form was the addition of arcades and aisles on either side of the nave, or central hall. Almost 700 years of consistency, and then, in less than 200 years, this form would evolve into the great Gothic cathedrals.

At a basic level, the structural system of an early medieval basilica consists of 2 walls and a series of trusses framing and supporting the roof. Each truss is a self-contained structural element, generating only vertical reactions at the supports, as opposed to the vertical and horizontal reactions of an arch. Downward loads are transmitted by the truss into the walls, then transmitted in axial compression through the walls and into the structural foundations. The walls, in effect, function as columns. They don't need to be particularly thick, but ideally the vertical load path should be uninterrupted. This limited the size and numbers of windows—and therefore, the amount of light—in these early structures.

By the 11th century, European builders were studying great Roman ruins and Byzantine structures and began incorporating these elements into their designs. This emerging Romanesque style is seen in the nave arches and groin-vaulted ceilings. With vaults came the addition of engaged columns on the interior walls and piers to support them. The problem with this arrangement was that the stone arches were heavy and the engaged columns very tall and slender, so they didn't much help to offset the arches' lateral thrust. Thickened sections were added to churches' walls to strengthen the vertical load path and to help the walls resist tipping and lateral bending. The thickened sections are called buttresses. These structural needs create the overall impression of strength and solidity in Romanesque architecture.

© Hemera/Thinkstock.

The pointed arches of Gothic cathedrals approach the ideal parabolic shape, requiring less support than semicircular arches and thus allowing large windows.

Another interesting feature of Romanesque architecture is the relieving arch. Like the empty chambers above the King's Chamber in the Great Pyramid at Giza, a relieving arch's job is to channel compressive vertical force around a delicate structure beneath. In Romanesque basilicas, relieving arches allowed builders to place large windows—called clerestory windows—high in the nave walls, diverting the weight of the vaults around them. Romanesque builders actually borrowed the relieving arch directly from Roman buildings.

The Gothic style gradually emerged from the Romanesque in northern Europe in the late 12th century. In general terms, the structural system is similar to that of a Romanesque basilica, but in detail the Gothic emphasized height and light, featuring ever-taller naves, pierced by ever-larger clerestory windows, and delineated by ever-more-slender engaged columns, all of which increased the tendency for lateral thrust to overturn the supporting walls.

Gothic builders met this challenge first and foremost with the pointed arch, which they adopted from Islamic architecture. The pointed arch generates significantly less lateral thrust than a semicircular one because it can approach the ideal, stable parabolic shape; therefore, it can be thinner as well, further decreasing the thrust. Secondly, ribs were added to the groined vaults to stiffen them and help transmit the weight to the engaged columns more effectively; this allowed for thinner vaults, reducing their weight and, once again, their lateral thrust. These 2 innovations were not enough to guarantee the columns' stability, however. So rather than use the traditional Romanesque buttress, which limited the size of the windows, Gothic builders detached these supports from the walls, creating the flying buttress. Finally, they added pinnacles to the tops of the flying buttresses, adding to their weight and therefore to their stability.

Viewed holistically, the ribbed vaults, pointed arches, slender columns, and flying buttresses of the Gothic cathedral created a fundamentally new type of structural system: a stone skeleton. Medieval builders finally surpassed the Romans in structural sophistication, and their stone skeletons presage the iron and steel skeleton construction of the 19th century and beyond. Amazingly, this system was developed empirically—entirely through trial and error—which ultimately limited what they could accomplish. ∎

Important Terms

apse: The semicircular end of a basilica or church.

buttress: A thickened section of a wall that resists the lateral thrust of ceiling vaults.

clerestory: The uppermost level of a nave, containing a row of large windows.

flying buttress: A structural element that resists the lateral thrust of ceiling vaults in a Gothic building. Flying buttresses are entirely external to the nave of the building they are supporting.

nave: The central hall of a church.

pinnacle: A pointed masonry element placed on top of a buttress.

relieving arch: An arch built into a wall above a door or window opening to divert compressive force around the opening.

Suggested Reading

Addis, *Building*, chap. 2.

Favier, *The World of Chartres*, chap. 6.

Gordon, *Structures*, chap. 9.

Nuttgens, *The Story of Architecture*, chaps. 9, 10, and 12.

Salvadori, *Why Buildings Stand Up*, chap. 12.

Questions to Consider

1. What is the relationship between form, function, and structure in a Gothic cathedral?*

2. Is a buttress a column or a beam?*

3. Which one of the four major Gothic-era structural innovations (pointed arches, ribbed vaulting, flying buttresses, and pinnacles) was most effective in stabilizing church naves against the overturning effect of lateral thrust?*

4. What does the collapse of the Cathedral of Saint-Pierre at Beauvais tell us about how medieval builders developed engineering expertise and construction methods?

Three Great Domes—Rome to the Renaissance
Lecture 13

This is a really interesting case of democracy in action: We have a popular assembly being used to determine the configuration of a major architectural feature in the city. ... Of course, democracies are not always known for their good judgment; and though this popular assembly decided to create a dome, at that time no one actually knew how such a dome might be built, and so the building sat, domeless, for 50 years.

The dome has existed since prehistoric times, at least as far back as 6000 B.C., but like arches, they didn't come of age until the Roman era. Their development was not gradual but marked by a few dramatic leaps in structural sophistication. As a structural element, a dome exhibits a unique pattern of internal forces. Along its **meridians**—that is, from apex to edge—a dome behaves much like an arch: Its self-weight causes lateral thrust and tends to flatten the dome out. Around its latitudinal **parellels**—that is, around the dome's circumference—the dome's self-weight causes tension, called **hoop stress**.

Hoop stress allows a dome to carry load without the sort of external lateral support you need for an arch, but only if the dome is made of a material capable of carrying load in tension. Unfortunately, the great dome builders of the ancient, Byzantine, and Renaissance eras did not have such materials. Their domes needed substantial external lateral support from all directions, and they developed several different methods for delivering that support.

The Pantheon, a Roman temple built by the architect Apollodorus around A.D. 126, consists of a 21-ft-thick cylindrical wall, or **drum**, topped by a 5000-ton concrete dome with a 142-ft diameter. Besides the main entryway, the drum contains 7 large interior niches, where the walls are thinner. The dome has a circular opening at the top, called the **oculus**.

To make this system work, Apollodorus reduced the weight of the dome as much as possible, not only with coffers and the oculus but also by narrowing the dome walls from 21 ft thick at the base to 4 ft thick at the top. He also varied the type of aggregate in the dome's concrete—heavier and stronger at the base, lighter at the top; modern analysis suggests that this alone reduced stresses in the dome by more than 40%. The circular shape of the drum is inherently resistant to overturning, and the walls extend well above the base of the dome to increase their weight. Apollodorus also used relieving arches on the outer surface of the drum, right where the niches are located inside, to compensate for the thinner walls at these points. To counteract the hoop stress near the base of the dome, he added weight to the dome's bottom third in the form of stepped rings around the outer perimeter. Finally, the oculus is rimmed by a **compression ring**, a sort of 3-dimensional keystone that just happens to be hollow in the middle.

The remarkable dome of Hagia Sophia is a replacement; the original collapsed in an earthquake in the 6th century, in part due to its suboptimal, shallow shape.

Istanbul's Hagia Sophia is the world's finest example of Byzantine architecture, constructed in the early 6th century A.D. At 102 ft in diameter, its masonry dome is smaller than that of the Pantheon but is considerably higher above the floor. Its heavy meridional ribs, supported by exterior buttresses, allow a ring of 40 windows in the dome's base. The dome rests on 4 arches atop 4 massive stone columns. The 4 triangular spaces bounded by the base of the dome and the sides of each arch are filled in, forming a **pendentive**. They provide a beautiful, smooth transition from the circular dome to the square bay below and a smooth vertical flow of forces from the dome to the foundations.

The building's original dome was actually quite shallow, only 26 ft high, which minimized hoop stresses but increased its lateral thrust, which probably contributed to its collapse after a series of earthquakes in the mid-6th century. The replacement dome is twice as tall, closer to a hemisphere, but still has considerable lateral thrust. The pendentive cannot contain this thrust; instead, lateral support is provided by **semidomes** and semicircular bays on either side of the church's central bay. These are supported in turn by substantial buttress vaults and semicircular chapels outside the semicircular bays, fanning the load outward and downward into the foundations. Each step of this amazing, complicated load path spreads the load wider, reducing its intensity, and creates an incomparably open, grand interior space.

The cathedral of Santa Maria del Fiore in Florence is a late Gothic/early Renaissance structure whose most famous feature, its 125-ft-diameter brick dome, was designed by Filippo Brunelleschi. In designing the dome, Brunelleschi faced 4 unique challenges: to build the dome on top of a 30-ft-tall cupola, which made it particularly vulnerable to instability; to create an octagonal dome; to support a heavy stone lantern on top of the dome; and to do all this 170 ft above the floor of the cathedral without the help of any temporary centering.

Brunelleschi's solutions were as ingenious as they were effective. He designed a tall dome to reduce lateral thrust and to better support the lantern. He constructed the dome as 2 thin shells rather than a single solid monolith, tied together with a grid of 24 meridional ribs and 9 horizontal ribs. The horizontal ribs were arched, effectively embedding a circular dome completely inside the exterior octagonal shell. He also included 3 stone and 1 timber horizontal chains to act as hoops, counteracting the hoop stress.

But Brunelleschi's most spectacular achievement was construction of the dome without temporary centering. As the dome grew taller, he kept the freshly set bricks from sliding inward and off their bed of wet mortar by using a herringbone brick pattern. For each course of masonry, the vertical bricks project above the most recent horizontal bricks, wedging the horizontal bricks in place. The entire construction process was aided by innovative, specialized machines that Brunelleschi designed for lifting and placing the components of the dome. We know about these devices today thanks to sketches by one of Brunelleschi's young apprentice engineers—Leonardo da Vinci. ■

Important Terms

compression ring: A ring of masonry used to reinforce the oculus of a dome.

drum: A cylindrical wall that supports a dome.

hoop stress: Tension stress occurring in the parallel direction in a dome.

meridian: A line of longitude on a dome.

oculus: A circular opening at the top of a dome.

parallel: A line of latitude on a dome.

pendentive: A triangular element used to provide a smooth transition from a square bay to the circular base of a dome.

semidome: A half dome.

Addis, *Building*, chaps. 1–3.

Fanelli and Fanelli, *Brunelleschi's Cupola*.

Nuttgens, *The Story of Architecture*, chaps. 8, 9, and 13.

Salvadori, *Why Buildings Stand Up*, chaps. 13–14.

Questions to Consider

1. What is the relationship between form, function, and structure in Brunelleschi's dome over the cathedral of Santa Maria del Fiore?*

2. Which of these 3 great domes do you consider to be most innovative?

3. The dome of the Pantheon can only be fully appreciated from inside the building. The dome of Santa Maria del Fiore is most appreciated (and best loved) for its exterior appearance. What structural features of the 2 domes contribute to this distinction?*

4. The dome of Hagia Sophia uses ribs and buttresses to allow for window openings at its base. Where else have we seen the use of ribs and buttresses to facilitate larger window openings?*

5. How would you compare these 3 domes with the dome of the Treasury of Atreus in Mycenae?

How Iron and Science Transformed Arch Bridges
Lecture 14

The circular iron spandrels in the Coalbrookdale Bridge are an example of that same phenomenon that we saw in ancient Greek temple architecture: the decorative stone triglyphs that represent the timber beams used in earlier wooden temples. The circular members at Coalbrookdale are actually artifacts carried over from an earlier structural form, even though they don't really make structural sense when they're implemented in iron.

Between the dawn of the Industrial Revolution and the present day, the development of the arch was most apparent in bridges. Two factors had the greatest impact on arch bridge development: the adoption of iron as a structural material and the introduction of true science-based design. Iron, of course, had been in general use for thousands of years, but prior to the Industrial Revolution, it was expensive and hard to produce in bulk. When the 18th-century British iron master Abraham Darby developed a process to use **coke** as fuel for smelting iron, the material became available in large batches and high quality for the first time.

Abraham Darby III, grandson of the iron master, secured a contract to build an iron bridge (the world's first) across the Severn River at Coalbrookdale, England, in 1777. The cast-iron structure with stone foundations was completed in 1779. The main arch spans 100 ft and is 40 ft high. It uses 5 parallel sets of arch ribs, each with a solid rectangular cross-section of iron measuring 9 × 7 in. The structure was assembled on a traditional temporary centering, and it was done in just 3 months; a stone bridge would have taken far longer to build.

The main external loads on the bridge are then transmitted downward from the **deck** through 2 different load paths: down through the vertical posts near the ends of the span and laterally into the arch rings near center of the span, both in compression. This design takes advantage of cast iron's properties—strong in compression, weak in tension. Many of the bridge's design elements are analogous to traditional stone arches: The links that align and brace the

73

arch rings resemble voussoir joints; the circular members serve as spandrels. All of the bridge's connections use traditional timber joinery methods; no one had yet considered making structural connections in iron. Overall, the structural system works identically to that of the Roman Pont Saint Martin. Darby designed his iron structure to mimic the known properties of masonry ones. It is the product of empirical design.

It took almost 200 years from Isaac Newton's discovery of the laws of motion to engineers' adoption of science-based design. This was in part because empirical design worked, refined by thousands of years of trial and error. Practicing engineers saw mathematical engineering as unnecessary at best, highly suspect at worst. But iron, being the first new structural material

© iStockphoto/Thinkstock.

The bridge at Coalbrookdale, England, was the world's first iron bridge, but it was designed using the principles of masonry bridge construction.

in about 2 millennia, had no empirical precedents to build on. So it's no coincidence that engineers turned to science just when they began using iron. Once they turned to science, the discipline developed rapidly. The Eads Bridge across the Mississippi River at St. Louis, Missouri, was designed in 1867—less than 100 years after Darby designed Coalbrookdale—using well-established, science-based engineering principles.

The Eads Bridge was James Eads's first bridge-building project. His masterpiece was the longest arch bridge in the world and the first to use steel as its primary structural material. Compared with Darby's bridge, the Eads Bridge is a far more structurally coherent design. The main arch ribs are hollow tubes rather than solid bars, because tubes are more resistant to buckling. Eads connected the arch ribs with trusses, and the spandrels are composed of vertical columns, which are simpler and more efficient than Darby's rings. Eads could not block river traffic with temporary centering during construction, so he devised a "canted lever" system for suspending the partially completed arches from temporary towers at the ends of each span— the origin of the term "**cantilever**." Many of Eads's ideas and techniques are still in use in some form today.

One of Eads's best-known contemporaries was French engineer Gustave Eiffel. Eiffel designed and built 7 major railroad bridges in the mountainous Massif Central region of southeastern France. The most magnificent and challenging of these was the Garabit Viaduct, completed in 1884. The structure was simple: a railroad line supported on a horizontal deck truss, which is supported on stone abutments at its ends, on the center of an arch in the middle, and a series of trussed towers in between.

The arch is the most remarkable feature. At 530 ft, it is 10 ft longer than the Eads Bridge's longest span, and at 400 ft high, it was the tallest arch in the world. Its shape is the optimum parabola, and rather than a solid girder, it is a truss, minimizing wind load. The top and bottom chords of the truss are crescent shaped, widest at the middle where internal moments are highest and tapering to points at the ends where internal moment is zero. It is optimally proportioned for both its self-weight and large, concentrated live loads crossing the span. Viewed in the context of traditional arch bridges, Eiffel's bridge has everything backward, but in terms of the underlying science, it's hard to imagine a more perfectly configured structure. In the Garabit Viaduct, we see science taking engineering in a whole new direction.

Today, Eiffel's arch has been refined even further. The Campo Volantin Bridge in Bilbao, Spain, designed by Santiago Calatrava and built in 1997, uses a **tied arch** that replaces heavy foundations with a tension tie that acts like a bowstring. This configuration opens up all sorts of possibilities, because the structural foundations no longer need to carry huge lateral thrust. The laterally curved deck is suspended by cable tension members off the side of the arch, in perfect counterbalance to it. The bridge's internal forces are so complex they could only be analyzed with the help of a computer, yet the underlying structural mechanics remain the same. ■

Important Terms

cantilever: (1) A beam supported at one end and unsupported at the other. The single support must prevent the supported end of the beam from rotating. (2) A construction technique in which halves of an arch or beam are temporarily suspended from the ends of the span until they can be joined in the center.

coke: A form of coal used as fuel in the manufacture of iron.

deck: A flat structural element that directly supports a floor, roof, or roadway.

sand casting: A process for manufacturing metal objects by using a mold made of compacted sand.

tied arch: An arch in which the lateral thrust is resisted by a tension member connecting the 2 ends of the arch together.

Suggested Reading

Billington, *The Tower and the Bridge*, chap. 8.

Gordon, *Structures*, chap. 10.

Petroski, *Engineers of Dreams*, chap. 2.

Lecture 14: How Iron and Science Transformed Arch Bridges

1. What are the relationships between form, function, and structure in the Eads Bridge?*

2. Modern structural design attempts to achieve cost effectiveness by minimizing weight. How did the advent of mass-produced iron contribute to this design philosophy? How did science contribute to this design philosophy?*

3. Why is the crescent shape of the Garabit Viaduct arch structurally optimal?*

Suspension Bridges—The Battle of the Cable
Lecture 15

As we study the early years of suspension bridge development, we'll see at least as many failures as successes. At some point, you may start to wonder why engineers even persisted with suspension bridges at all. After so many failures, it would have been entirely reasonable to just give up and try something else. The answer, I think, is that suspension bridges represent extraordinary potential for greatness.

For the better part of 2 centuries, the **suspension bridge** has been the most effective means of building across vast distances. On a typical suspension bridge, traffic loads are applied to its deck or decks, which are supported by **stiffening trusses** (or sometimes **stiffening girders**). The trusses hang from vertical cables called **suspenders**. The suspenders transmit the weight up to 2 or more main cables, the principal load-carrying elements of the bridge. The cables are held aloft by towers; where the cable drapes over the tower, it transmits load downward, into the foundations. Each cable must also be anchored to the earth at each end to maintain its tension.

The first persistent challenge in suspension bridge design is constructing the main cables and their **anchorages**; the second is controlling the bridge's inherent susceptibility to vibrations caused by wind. In this lecture, we'll focus on the development of cables and anchorages; the following lecture will discuss the more protracted struggle against wind.

In 1801, James Finley built the very first suspension bridge capable of carrying vehicular traffic: Jacob's Creek Bridge in western Pennsylvania. Finley was a justice of the peace, not an engineer, and his bridges did not stand the test of time. But his longest span, a 308-ft pedestrian bridge across the Schuylkill River in Philadelphia, collapsed during a snowstorm only 8 years after it was built. Many Finley bridges have collapsed, and most have been replaced. But despite these failures, the idea of suspension bridges caught on.

Around the same period, Britain's Royal Navy engineers had developed the **eyebar chain** as a potential replacement for rope rigging. An eyebar chain consists of flat iron bars with a hole at each end, connected with iron pins. (A bicycle chain is a common example of an eyebar chain.) Eyebar chains could be constructed of a stack of eyebars—that is, they can easily be made structurally redundant—so British engineers to begin experimenting with the eyebar chain in suspension bridges. In 1817, Royal Navy officer Samuel Brown developed and patented a system of eyebar chains and incorporated them into the first British suspension bridge capable of carrying vehicular traffic: the Union Bridge over the Tweed River at New Waterford. Its arrangement established the general pattern for British suspension bridge development for the next 50 years; the Union Bridge was so well built that it still carries vehicular traffic today.

Library of Congress, Prints and Photographs Division.

John Roebling's Brooklyn Bridge, completed in the 1880s, is supported by a cable system still used in suspension bridges today.

In 1818, Scottish engineer Thomas Telford created the Menai Strait Bridge in northwestern Wales. It has a 579-ft central span suspended from 2 massive limestone towers. The main cables are 16 wrought-iron eyebar chains, each composed of more than 900 individual eyebars. Although Telford disdained math and scientific theory, he was also a strong believer in experimentation. He conducted extensive laboratory tests on the chains and designed the bridge such that the chains would never exceed 1/3 of their ultimate strength. The Menai Strait Bridge, still in service today, established the eyebar chain as the preferred configuration for suspension bridges in Britain.

The French developed an interest in suspension bridges after Claude Navier visited the U.S. in the 1820s to study American developments in suspension bridge design. His 1823 report was the world's first theoretical treatment of suspension bridges. French engineers soon began experimenting with wire cables rather than iron chains, and Swiss engineer Guillaume Henri Dufour constructed the world's first permanent wire-cable suspension bridge in 1823. Dufour's cables were bundles of hundreds of parallel wires, not twisted wires as many believe.

Iron and steel wires are stronger than eyebars, and the cable bundles offer greater redundancy, so in theory, cables are superior to eyebar chains. In practice, the effectiveness of a wire cable depends on all the wires carrying approximately equal tension and on how well the cables are anchored at each end. Early bridges were built by prefabricating the cables on the ground, which could compromise the cable's strength by stretching some wires too tightly while leaving others slack.

In theory, cables are superior to eyebar chains. In practice, the effectiveness of a wire cable depends on all the wires carrying approximately equal tension.

In 1844, German American bridge pioneer John Roebling devised a system for fabricating cables in place on the bridge while building the Allegheny Aqueduct in Pittsburgh. A single iron or steel wire is looped across the bridge hundreds of times around a **strand shoe** at each anchorage. The wire is pulled back and forth from anchorage to anchorage, over the towers, by means of a winch and **traveler** wheel on an iron or steel haul rope, until the cable strand reaches the required thickness. With all **strands** in position, cables are compacted with a circular clamp, wrapped tightly with fine wire, and coated with weather-resistant paint. In Roebling's Brooklyn Bridge cables, for example, each strand consists of 278 individual wires and 19 strands, bundled to form a single main cable of more than 5000 wires. Roebling patented this system in 1847; it has been used, with only minor modifications, on every major suspension bridge since.

This system conquered the even-tension problem. Anchorages, however, were still susceptible to failure due to corrosion of the wires at each end. Roebling addressed this problem by attaching the strand shoes to corrosion-resistant eyebar chains, then attaching the chains to the anchorage, which was situated at the bottom of a pit, then filled with enough stone masonry to counterbalance the largest tension force the cable would ever carry. This system, with minor variations, was used in the Brooklyn Bridge and virtually every other suspension bridge built since. It turns out that neither an eyebar chain nor a cable alone is the best system for suspension bridge construction; the ideal configuration includes both. ■

Important Terms

anchorage: A structure that connects the main cables of a suspension bridge to the earth.

eyebar chain: A chain composed of iron or steel bars linked together with pins.

saddle: An iron or steel element that guides the main cables of a suspension bridge across the tops of the towers.

stiffening girder: A beam that directly supports the deck of a suspension bridge while resisting wind-induced vibration and distortion of the cable due to concentrated loads.

stiffening truss: A truss that directly supports the deck of a suspension bridge while resisting wind-induced vibration and distortion of the cable due to concentrated loads.

strand: A bundle of parallel wires constituting a component of the main cable of a suspension bridge. Each cable is composed of multiple strands, and each strand is composed of multiple wires.

strand shoe: A horseshoe-shaped fitting that connects one strand of a suspension bridge cable to its anchorage.

suspender: A vertical cable that connects the stiffening truss or stiffening girder to a main cable in a suspension bridge.

suspension bridge: A structure in which the deck is supported on or beneath two or more draped cables.

traveler: A device used to fabricate suspension bridge cables in place on the bridge by pulling individual loops of wire across the span one at a time.

Suggested Reading

Billington, *The Tower and the Bridge*, chaps. 2.

McCullough, *The Great Bridge*, chaps. 15–19.

Peters, *Transitions in Engineering*, chaps. 2–6.

Questions to Consider

1. What is the relationship between form, function, and structure in the George Washington Bridge? Is this relationship the same for all bridges?*

2. Why are wire cables theoretically superior to eyebar chains for suspension bridge cables?*

3. How is our understanding of the world's great suspension bridges enhanced by learning how the cables were constructed?*

4. Do you think that frequent failures of early suspension bridges should have dissuaded engineers from continuing to develop this structural configuration?

Suspension Bridges—The Challenge of Wind
Lecture 16

"For a few moments we watched [the Wheeling Bridge] with breathless anxiety, lunging like a ship in a storm; at one time it rose to nearly the height of the tower, then fell, and twisted and writhed, and was dashed almost bottom upward. At last there seemed to be a determined twist along the entire span ... and down went the immense structure from its dizzy height to the stream below, with an appalling crash and roar."
— The Wheeling *Intelligencer*, May 17, 1854

The Tacoma Narrows Bridge was the third-longest span in the world when it opened to traffic in July 1940. It collapsed just 4 months later in a steady 42-mph wind. Designed by Leon Moisseiff, one of America's leading bridge engineers, it used a well-established, 140-year-old structural configuration. How could a scientifically designed structure fail so catastrophically under such unremarkable loading conditions?

The earliest suspension bridges usually had unstiffened decks. In the 1820s, Guillaume Henri Dufour noted how concentrated live loads made such decks dip and distort, sometimes violently, due to the inherent flexibility of the cable as a structural form: As the load on a cable changes, the shape changes to preserve equilibrium. Dufour also noticed that unstiffened decks are extremely susceptible to vibrations. In longitudinal vibration, one side of the bridge deck moves downward and the opposite side rises. In **torsion**, the bridge deck twists from side to side. The latter happened to the Tacoma Narrows Bridge just before its collapse.

Dufour's tests were impeccable, but his conclusions were fundamentally flawed: Dufour decided to combat vibration by making the bridge heavier (that is, increasing its mass in accordance with Newton's second law). Many engineers concurred. But this reasoning only addressed half of the problem. A heavy object will accelerate less than a light one, but it will accelerate, and once it's in motion, it is more resistant to deceleration as well. Newton's second law is a double-edged sword.

Under certain conditions, a bridge deck vibrating in torsional mode can experience **aeroelastic flutter**. When moving air interacts with the elastic structure, each oscillation tends to make the next oscillation larger. Such flutter is strongly influenced by the shape and proportions of the bridge deck. Also, for any given shape, there's a characteristic wind speed at which flutter is most likely to occur. Finally, the effect of flutter is far more severe if the bridge deck is torsionally flexible. The best way to prevent excessive vibration in a suspension bridge is not to make it heavier but to make it stiffer. Even after stiffening trusses became commonplace engineering practice, the belief in mass as a good substitute for stiffening persisted, with sometimes catastrophic results. The collapse of the Wheeling Bridge in May 1854 was no doubt the result of this mistaken assumption.

The Niagara Gorge Bridge, designed by John Roebling, dispelled the common belief that suspension bridges couldn't be used as railroad bridges because of the weight of locomotives. Ironically, John Roebling had made a name for

The trusses beneath the Golden Gate Bridge are not merely decorative; they help the deck resist wind and other live loads.

© iStockphoto/Thinkstock.

himself building aqueduct suspension bridges, which don't require stiffening because the weight of the water flowing through the aqueduct channel is perfectly uniform. Unbalanced loading is essentially impossible. His system uses a belt-and-suspenders approach—that is, 2 independent systems each capable of stabilizing the bridge on its own: first, very deep iron stiffening trusses, and second, 2 sets of iron stay cables, one radiating from the towers down to the tops of the stiffening trusses and the other anchored on the cliffs below and radiating to the bottoms of the trusses. This system worked well against wind as well as traffic loads and was used in Roebling's other bridges, including the Brooklyn Bridge.

It's clear that Roebling's solution was on some level an empirical one; the dynamic behavior of a suspension bridge due to wind loading was simply too complex for the analytical tools of the era to predict reliably. Over time, as scientific methods improved and engineers' reliance on them increased, empirical methods faded from view, and bridge engineers somehow forgot Roebling's successful system. Their confidence in the state of the engineering art would prove unfounded.

In the 1920s and 1930s, Leon Moisseiff achieved great notoriety by developing a new science-based methodology for suspension bridge design called deflection theory. One of the principal implications of this theory was that long-span suspension bridges don't require stiffening trusses because their mass stabilized them against wind-induced vibration. For some reason, the bridge-engineering community accepted this theory, even though it had been so thoroughly discredited in practice. Moisseiff applied his deflection theory in the Tacoma Narrows Bridge, using a light, shallow stiffening girder under the deck, rather than more robust trusses.

We already know how this story ends. We know today that Moisseiff's theory was an oversimplification that failed to account for the complex interactions between the flow of air around a bridge deck and the dynamic response of the structural system. Today, this case has become a symbol of the dangers of arrogance born of overconfidence in science-based design methods, and belt-and-suspenders engineering has made a bit of a comeback.

The late 20th century saw dramatic new approaches to dealing with wind effects in suspension bridge design, enabled in part by wind-tunnel technologies and highly sophisticated computer models. One of the most spectacular products of this effort is the Severn Bridge in Britain. Originally designed with a stiffening truss, it was redesigned after poor performance of a scale model in wind-tunnel testing. The trusses were replaced with a new aerodynamic box girder, which resists wind-induced vibration by virtue of its aerodynamic shape and is inherently resistant to torsion. Also, the suspenders are not vertical but V-shaped, effectively turning the cable system into a truss. The result is enhanced stiffness without sacrificing graceful, slender lines. With the construction of the Severn Bridge, the battle against the wind has finally been won. ■

Important Terms

aeroelastic flutter: A phenomenon in which an elastic body oscillates in response to air moving across it.

torsion: Twisting of a structural element.

Suggested Reading

McCullough, *The Great Bridge*, chaps. 15–19.

Salvadori, *Why Buildings Stand Up*, chap. 10.

Salvadori and Levy, *Why Buildings Fall Down*, chap. 7.

Van der Zee, *The Gate*.

Questions to Consider

1. How did science-based design contribute to the collapse of the Tacoma Narrows Bridge?

2. How did the collapse of the Tacoma Narrows Bridge contribute to science-based design?

3. What lessons can we learn about engineering innovation from the development of the Severn Bridge?*

4. Which suspension bridge do you consider to be most aesthetically pleasing? Why?

Great Cantilever Bridges—Tragedy and Triumph
Lecture 17

The Firth of Forth Bridge is often cited not only as the world's strongest bridge, but also as the world's most expensive bridge. But from the perspective of the North British Railway, I think it's fair to say that money was no object. As Thomas Bouch learned, you can't put a price tag on public trust.

On December 28, 1879, the Firth of Tay Bridge in Scotland collapsed in a gale, killing all 75 occupants of a train that was crossing the bridge at that moment. This tragedy triggered a series of events that dramatically altered the course of bridge design in both Britain and the United States and ultimately prompted the design and construction of 2 of the world's great structures.

The original Tay Bridge was the longest in the world on its completion in 1878. It was a 2-mi-long series of 11 iron high girders—also known as **through trusses**—and 74 **deck trusses** simply supported on cast-iron piers. The high girders, each 245 ft long, were located in the center of the navigation channel. A little over a year later, when that gale struck, all 11 high girders collapsed. Planning for a new Tay Bridge began shortly after the disaster, and a far more robust structure with much heavier trusses and piers opened in 1887. In the wake of these events, John Fowler and his assistant, Benjamin Baker, were appointed the principal engineers for the nearby Firth of Forth Bridge project in 1881. Discarding simply supported spans as too weak and continuous spans as too hard to execute safely over such long distances, they designed the bridge as a cantilever truss.

A cantilever bridge avoids the principal limitation of a continuous-span bridge—its susceptibility to stresses caused by support settlements. If a support moves, the bridge is articulated, so it can accommodate that movement. A cantilever bridge also has a similar level of structural efficiency to a continuous span bridge because it still bends in negative curvature over the supports and in positive curvature near the center of the span. Nonetheless, the Firth of Forth site would require 2 spans of an unprecedented 1700 ft each. It was a poor site for a simply supported or continuous span, having no firm ground to build supports on at midstream. A suspension bridge might have been an option, but the discredited designer of the Firth of Tay Bridge, Thomas Bouch, had proposed a suspension bridge for the site; any bridge that resembled his plans would have been a public relations disaster. A cantilever was the only viable option. To build up public confidence in his cantilever design for the Firth of Forth Bridge, Baker created an ingenious visual representation of the cantilever system, constructed entirely with human beings.

"Cantilever" refers to any structural element with one unsupported end. The most common configuration for cantilever bridges has 2 exterior supports called abutments and 2 interior supports called piers. Construction starts with the 2 end spans, with the **anchor arm** of the span fixed at the foundation and the **cantilever arm** of the span unsupported. To keep the cantilever arm from collapsing, the anchor arm must be counterweighted to keep the span at equilibrium. The **suspended span** is placed between the cantilevered end spans. In a way, the center span is a simply supported truss. The Firth of

Cantilever bridges (background) and suspension bridges (foreground) are the best options for spanning long distances.

Forth Bridge is composed of 3 cantilever units, with 2 suspended spans in between. The piers spread outward at their bases to provide stability with respect to wind loads. The profile of the main truss is deepest over the piers and in the center of the suspended span, where maximum internal moments are likely to occur.

Fowler and Baker designed the Firth of Forth Bridge not just to be strong but also to look strong. Its individual structural elements are huge; for example, the bottom chords of the cantilever arms are steel tubes 12 ft in diameter. The bridge was also the world's first structure to be made entirely of steel, which is 50% stronger than wrought iron. This distinction from the Tay Bridge also helped ease the public's fears.

Opinions about the aesthetics of the Firth of Forth Bridge are sharply divided, and some engineers consider it structurally excessive—inefficient and wasteful. But the high cost of the structure proved to be a wise long-term investment, and aesthetically pleasing or not, it's hard to imagine a more beautiful marriage of form, function, and structure.

One critic of the Forth Bridge was a prominent American engineer named Theodore Cooper. He called it "the clumsiest structure ever designed by man" and boasted that American engineers were capable of designing lighter, more elegant structures. His supervision of a bridge across the St. Lawrence River near Quebec City, Canada, would prove his boasting unfounded. His arrogance, slipshod work, and denial of facts reported to him by his site engineer led to the collapse of a cantilever arm under construction, killing 75 workers. The main cause of the error was a design flaw: When he had directed that the main span be increased from 1600 to 1800 ft—ostensibly for structural reasons, but perhaps to usurp the Forth's record as the world's longest bridge span—the initial estimates of dead load were never adjusted. Cooper did not cause the error, but he did not catch it in his review of the plans either. As chief engineer, he ultimately shouldered the responsibility, and the blame.

The aftermath of the Quebec Bridge collapse was eerily similar to the aftermath of the Tay Bridge collapse. In both cases, though the failure was a case of engineer negligence, public confidence in the associated structural configuration was shaken. As a result, no new cantilever structures were built in North America for nearly 20 years.

What should we learn from these stories? First, that engineering is an inherently human endeavor profoundly influenced by human aspirations and human creativity, but also by human frailty; and second, that design isn't always based on objective engineering criteria but also influenced by public perception. ∎

Important Terms

anchor arm: The portion of a cantilever bridge that counterbalances the cantilever arm.

cable-stayed bridge: A bridge supported by straight cables radiating outward from one or more towers.

cantilever arm: The portion of a cantilever bridge that projects beyond an intermediate support.

deck truss: A truss bridge with the deck located at the level of the top chord.

suspended span: A central span of a cantilever bridge. The suspended span is supported by the cantilever arms.

through truss: A truss bridge with the deck located at the level of the bottom chord.

Suggested Reading

Billington, *The Tower and the Bridge*, chap. 8.

Petroski, *Engineers of Dreams*, chap. 3.

Winpenny, *Without Fitting, Filing, or Chipping*, chap. 6.

1. In designing a structure, what is the engineer's ethical responsibility to the general public? How should this responsibility be balanced against the needs of the client and the desire for innovation in design?

2. To what extent should public perceptions about safety be taken into account in the design of great structures?

3. What can the Quebec Bridge disaster teach us about the influence of the design-construction organization on the success of a major project?

4. How can the engineer's inherent human fallibility be accounted for in the design of complex systems?*

The Rise of Iron- and Steel-Framed Buildings
Lecture 18

> Despite their plain appearance and utilitarian origins, these early British mill buildings are some of the world's great structures—in part because they're important milestones in a developmental process that will ultimately lead us to the modern skyscraper, but also because they're innovative structures in their own right.

A frame is an assembly of structural elements that supports a building in the same way that a skeleton supports the human body. A frame is not a truss; in a truss, all structural elements carry load either in axial tension or compression. In a frame, at least one member carries load in flexure. The 2 basic types of frames are **rigid frames** and **braced frames**. Rigid frames attain their stability from **rigid connections**; members always retain their relationship with respect to each other. Braced frames have diagonal bracing, giving the frame lateral stability. Without bracing, the frame cannot carry load, because the frame's connections are not rigid. Braced frames are similar to trusses because they take advantage of the inherent stability of the triangle. But braced frames still carry some load in flexure, so they are not quite the same as trusses.

While the great Gothic cathedrals of medieval France were constructed with stone frames, the 18th century saw the advent of iron-frame construction. The Théâtre Français, built in 1790 in Paris, was probably the world's first public building designed to be fully fire resistant; most of its resistant elements were stone and terra-cotta, but the interior columns were cast iron, and the building used the world's first wrought-iron roof trusses. Before wrought iron came along, wood was the only construction material capable of carrying significant tension, so the use of iron trusses and beams constituted an improvement in fire resistance.

The decisive stimulus for the systematic integration of iron into building structures was the rapid growth of the textile industry in Britain during the mid-18th century. Most mill buildings used brick masonry exterior walls, but the floors, beams, and columns were made of wood.

Mills were filled with highly flammable fibers and lubricating oils, and the mill machinery sparked during operation. Under these conditions, fires were inevitable and potentially devastating. Also, the division of most mill structures into identical **bays** meant cost savings in using standardized, optimized structural elements in their construction.

There is a clear path from Chatham Dockyard to the Empire State Building.

The earliest comprehensive iron framing system was devised by William Strutt for his mill at Derby in 1793. It **cruciform** cast-iron columns supported wooden beams that were sheathed in iron to improve their fire resistance. The floors consisted of jack arches—flat brick vaults supported on bevels added to the sides of the beam—and iron tie rods were used to restrain the jack arches' thrust. Above the jack arches was a layer of sand, topped with a brick tile floor. This was an exceptionally well-conceived structural system in its own right, but it also served as the jump-off point for a series of progressively more effective innovations. Charles Bage's mill at Shrewsbury replaced the iron-wrapped wooden beams with cast iron and thus created the world's first fully integrated iron-framed building. Bage also broke new ground by using simple mechanics theory to calculate the required size for the columns, possibly the first time in history that scientific theory was applied to the design of a structural element.

This mill design was steadily refined and reached its peak in Orrell's Mill, constructed in 1834. Designed by ironmaster William Fairbairn and mathematician Eaton Hodgkinson, its cast-iron columns have hollow circular cross-sections, and the jack arches' tie rods are embedded within the arches to improve both fire resistance and appearance. But its most impressive element is its asymmetrical I-beams. The beam's shape takes advantage of cast iron's strength in compression by reducing the size of the top (compressed) flange to save weight and materials. The beam's profile is parabolic—deeper at mid-span, where internal moment is strongest. Hodgkinson's mathematically designed beams reduced the cost of iron in Orrell's Mill by 20%–30% and demonstrated the value of science-based design.

Although these British mill buildings used innovative iron framing inside, all of them used traditional masonry outer walls. These walls were also structural elements: bearing walls carrying a portion of the load from the floors and the roof to foundations in axial compression, just like columns. The next logical step was to replace these masonry walls with iron. In the 1840s, Daniel Badger earned considerable notoriety for his cast iron facades, which he installed on many buildings in New York City, like the E. V. Haughwout Building of 1857. All 4 walls of the Watervliet Arsenal are cast iron and are fully integrated within a well-conceived system of iron roof trusses, columns, and beams. These iron walls carry load in exactly the same way as the masonry walls they replaced. Among the first buildings to use fully iron-framed structural systems were British Royal Navy ship sheds at the Chatham Dockyard in Kent. There, the iron members carry all of the loads; the walls are just in-fill. If you can see and understand structure, you can see there is a clear path from Chatham Dockyard to the Empire State Building.

As a building gets taller, load-bearing exterior walls must necessarily get thicker in order to ensure their stability. When the building height approaches about 10 stories, the walls will inevitably become so thick that they begin to impinge on the floor space of the building. So the final step in the development of a fully iron-framed structural system was replacement of the solid iron wall with iron columns and beams. Integrated iron framing allowed engineers to maximize floor space with thinner walls and taller structures, as well as to maximize natural lighting with large windows. The need for efficiency put engineering front and center in the design process at last. The age of the skyscraper had begun. ∎

Important Terms

bay: A rectangular module of a frame structure, formed by 4 columns.

braced frame: A frame that obtains its stability from diagonal bracing members or shear walls. A braced frame normally has pinned connections.

cruciform: Cross-shaped; this term is usually applied to the cross-section of a structural element.

frame: A structure composed of multiple members, at least one of which carries load in flexure.

pinned connection: A connection that allows the connected structural elements to rotate with respect to each other.

rigid connection: A connection that restrains the connected structural elements from rotating with respect to each other.

rigid frame: A frame that obtains its stability from rigid connections between the beams and columns.

shear wall: A type of lateral bracing consisting of a reinforced concrete or masonry wall filling in one or more bays of the frame.

Suggested Reading

Addis, *Building*, chaps. 5–7.

Billington, *The Tower and the Bridge*, chap. 7.

Dupre, *Skyscrapers*, p. 13–21.

Smith and Coull, *Tall Building Structures*, chap. 4.

Questions to Consider

1. What is the relationship between form, function, and structure in the iron-framed British textile mills of the Industrial Revolution?*

2. What conditions and circumstances stimulated innovation in the design of iron-frame buildings?

3. Why should the early British mill buildings be considered great structures?*

4. Why did the development of iron-framed exterior walls lag behind the development of interior iron framing by about 50 years?*

The Great Skyscraper Race
Lecture 19

In 1st-century Rome, emperors constructed grand public buildings to win the favor of the masses and to symbolize imperial power. In 12th-century Europe, the Catholic Church built grand cathedrals to glorify God and place religion at the very center of everyday life. In early 20th-century America, corporations built grand skyscrapers to demonstrate the power of capitalism and to symbolize national aspirations for world leadership.

The precursors of the skyscraper—textile mills, ship sheds, and the like—were innovative largely out of utility. In Chicago during the 1870s, the need for commercial development after the Great Fire provided the same sort of impetus, so it's not surprising that many commercial high-rise buildings of the period were innovative in design yet simple and utilitarian in appearance. The exterior of William LeBaron Jenney's First Leiter Building of 1879 consists of little more than beams and columns with windows in between; form follows structure. Jenney's work and that of his Chicago contemporaries—Daniel Burnham, Louis Sullivan, John Root, and others—was so influential that it was branded the **Chicago School** of architecture.

The Chicago School's buildings were characterized by iron- or steel-framed structural systems, nonstructural facade walls, large windows, and little external ornamentation. Louis Sullivan, one of the most eloquent voices of the school, said "form ever follows function." Sullivan's 1891 Wainwright Building in St. Louis illustrates this maxim perfectly. It was the first all-steel building frame in the United States, but more important, it follows a tripartite division that reflects the internal use of the building: Large windows, a decorative facade, and an open, welcoming main entrance on the bottom stories, which have the most interaction with the public; a series of identical office floors with identical divisions inside and an identical grid of windows outside; and a plain attic on top, with few or no windows. Aesthetically, the facade is often likened to the divisions of a classical Greek column, though this look has no relationship to how the structural system works.

The Wainwright Building and its contemporaries weren't designed with wind loads in mind, although their rigid frames do resist lateral loads. As buildings grew taller and facades tended toward more glass and less masonry, engineers began explicitly considering the effect of wind loads in their designs. One of the first buildings to use a fully integrated, scientifically designed system for resisting wind loads was the Metropolitan Life Tower in New York City. Its frame becomes lighter, and incidentally less rigid, the higher the building rises, but at any given level, a bracing system only needs to carry the total wind load above that level. Cumulative wind load actually decreases with height.

Unlike the forward-looking, functionally driven designs of the Chicago School, the skyscrapers of New York borrowed architectural styles from earlier ages to satisfy the egos of corporate titans. They wanted headquarters

The simple-looking exteriors of Chicago School buildings conceal the innovative structural elements that make them the world's first true skyscrapers.

that symbolized their power, and the ultimate expression of power was height. During an amazing 23-year period, sometimes called the Great Skyscraper Race, the title "world's tallest" changed hands 6 times, starting with the 1908 Singer Building at 612 ft tall and ending with the 1931 Empire State Building, at almost exactly twice the height: 1250 ft tall. From an engineering perspective, the most important aspect of the race was that the buildings made no significant structural innovations. They were all direct applications of the skeleton framing system pioneered by William LeBaron Jenney in the 1870s.

For the next great innovation in structural design, we shift to Chicago in the 1960s at the birth of the **Second Chicago School**. Fazlur Khan, a Bangladeshi American structural engineer, recognized that the traditional system for resisting wind loads—a rigid grid of columns and beams at every floor—had become too expensive. His insight was to view a high-rise structure as if the entire building were one huge structural element resembling an upright cantilever beam. Knowing that a hollow tube is far more efficient than a solid bar in both bending and axial compression, he created the **framed-tube** system, in which a rigid external shell of beams and columns provides the building's lateral load-carrying capacity.

Since 1970, many designers have adopted Khan's "big picture" structural concept but implemented it in a variety of ways. Bruce Graham's 100-story John Hancock Center in Chicago uses a **trussed-tube** bracing system, which has 30% less steel than similarly tall buildings and saved perhaps $15 million in building costs. Graham and Khan also implemented a **bundled-tube** system in Chicago's Sears Tower, which was the world's tallest building for more than 20 years.

Not all of these new towers were quite so successful. New York's Citygroup Center uses a unique chevron bracing system, but its designer, William LeMessurier, didn't fully check its resistance to quartering winds until after the tower was built. He then discovered that, due to a combination of factors, the chevrons were being stressed at about 160% higher than predicted, and the tower could blow over in even a modest windstorm. LeMessurier blew the whistle on himself, and emergency repairs shored up the structural system. Despite LeMessurier's culpability, he was lauded as a hero for his integrity and his aggressive efforts to rectify his error.

The most famous application of Khan's framed-tube system was New York's World Trade Center, built in 1972. Each tower was a hollow tube composed of 47 heavy steel box columns per side. These columns were welded to steel beams at each floor, forming a rigid lattice. This shell carried the lateral wind load and a portion of the dead and occupancy loads. The remaining gravity loads were carried by a cluster of columns at the buildings' cores, which also housed the elevator shafts, stairwells, and utilities ducts. The configuration was architecturally successful, structurally efficient, and highly functional, but it would prove to be unexpectedly vulnerable to the terror attacks of September 11, 2001. The buildings survived the aircraft impact but could not withstand the effects of the fires that followed, which caused the floor trusses to sag and collapse. With the loss of each successive floor, the intact columns lost their bracing, reducing their strength until they buckled and collapsed. The World Trade Center tragedy showed, sadly, that a perfectly adequate structural design can be compromised when new conditions arise. ∎

Important Terms

bundled-tube system: A variation on the framed tube system that combines several framed tubes into a single structural system.

Chicago School: An architectural movement of the late 1800s and early 1900s that promoted the use of iron- and steel-frame structural systems in commercial buildings.

framed-tube system: A type of structural system used in modern skyscrapers of the Second Chicago School. In the framed-tube system, a rigid external shell of beams and columns provides the lateral load-carrying capacity of the structure.

Second Chicago School: An architectural movement that originated in the 1940s but was centered on Fazlur Khan's development of the framed-tube system for skyscraper design in the 1960s.

trussed-tube system: A variation on the framed-tube system. A trussed tube integrates diagonal braces into the exterior lateral load-carrying frame.

Suggested Reading

Addis, *Building*, chaps. 8–9.

Billington, *The Tower and the Bridge*, chap. 13.

Dupre, *Skyscrapers*.

Salvadori, *Why Buildings Stand Up*, chap. 7.

Salvadori and Levy, *Why Buildings Fall Down*, chap. 2.

Smith and Coull, *Tall Building Structures*, chap. 4.

Questions to Consider

1. What is the relationship between form and structure in the Empire State Building? In the John Hancock Center?*

2. In what ways did the development of skyscrapers in the early 20th century resemble the development of Egyptian pyramids, Roman basilicas, and Gothic cathedrals?*

3. What do the architectural embellishments of the Singer Building (designed in the Beaux-Arts style), the Met Life Tower (modeled on the medieval campanile of San Marco in Venice), and the Woolworth Building (a Neo-Gothic spire) tell us about the aspirations of their owners and designers?

4. Which of the 3 generations of skyscrapers do you find most interesting?

5. The skyscraper pictured below is the Bank of China Tower in Hong Kong, completed in 1990. How would you characterize its structural system?*

© iStockphoto/Thinkstock.

The Beauty and Versatility of Modern Concrete
Lecture 20

> The Ingalls Building was widely viewed as a very high-risk enterprise. Because of official skepticism, it took 2 years to get the building permit approved; and when construction was completed and the formwork was removed, one reporter stayed on site all night so that he'd be an eyewitness to the building's collapse. Needless to say, the Ingalls Building didn't collapse.

Concrete is the most commonly used construction material, so many of its uses tend to be mundane. It can also be used in exciting ways: Frank Lloyd Wright's Fallingwater; Robert Maillart's stunning Salginatobel Bridge; Pier Nervi's Palazzeto dello Sport in Rome; Sydney's famous opera house; the City of Arts and Sciences in Valencia; and the world's tallest building, the Burj Khalifa in Dubai. Concrete's best feature is its versatility.

The story of modern concrete technology begins in 1824 with the invention by Joseph Aspdin of Portland cement, which could be mass produced. Concrete first became popular as a replacement for stone foundations; by the 1850s, engineers were experimenting with concrete arch bridges and aqueducts. But the full potential of concrete wouldn't be realized until 1867, when a French gardener named Joseph Monier began making large flower pots using concrete reinforced with iron rods. He soon began experiments on concrete structural elements and devised a system for reinforcing concrete structural members with iron exactly where tension occurs. So, for example, a concrete beam, experiencing tension on the bottom, would be reinforced with metal or steel bars on its lower surface to carry some of the tension. Even if the **reinforced concrete** cracks, the tension is carried safely; in fact, cracks are a good sign, demonstrating that the full capacity of the steel is being used.

Whether in tension or compression, steel can only carry load if it is firmly bonded to the concrete. In the early years, the bars were square iron rods spiraled to grip the concrete. Modern structures use circular steel or iron rods with raised ridges to provide that same mechanical bond. Reinforcing bars are normally preassembled into a self-contained cage and placed inside the forms before the concrete is poured in. This creates a strong mechanical linkage between bars and concrete, creating an integrated structural unit.

In Europe and the United States, several entrepreneurs capitalized on Monier's work by developing comprehensive systems for reinforced concrete buildings. Most successful was François Hennebique, who patented the Hennebique system for providing fully integrated structural systems in France in 1892. Hennebique built few structures himself but licensed his technology to contractors and monitored their methods for quality. By 1909, 20,000 Hennebique structures had been built worldwide. In the U.S., reinforced concrete was pioneered by Ernest Ransome, who developed a system similar to Hennebique's in the late 1800s. In 1903, Ransome's system was used in the world's first reinforced concrete skyscraper: the Ingalls Building in Cincinnati. At 16 stories, it was only about half as tall as the tallest steel-framed building at that time; nonetheless, it was a groundbreaking building in terms of its structure. Other architects and engineers began experimenting with new forms uniquely tailored to concrete. The Art Nouveau church of Saint-Jean de Montmartre in Paris was one of the world's first noncommercial reinforced concrete buildings. Its slender arches and vaults couldn't have been built with traditional masonry.

As Maillart demonstrated, a sincere form is also often an economical one.

More than any other early 20th-century structure, the Salginatobel Bridge in the Swiss Alps reflects the unique qualities of reinforced concrete. Maillart pioneered hollow concrete box girders in the Zuoz Bridge in 1901. When its spandrel walls began to crack, Maillart proved that the cracks didn't affect the structural integrity of the bridge; they weren't even part of the main load path. Realizing that he could remove most of the material in the spandrels in future designs led him to the design of the Salginatobel Bridge. While the concept behind it is the same as Eiffel's Garabit Viaduct, the members are designed for the smaller span and the qualities of concrete: Its 3 arch segments are thick in the middle and thin toward the arch hinges to act as both compression members and beams. Note that when the bridge was designed, the government's sole criterion was low cost; Maillart also aimed for "sincerity of form," a physical configuration that communicates how the bridge carries load. As Maillart demonstrated, a sincere form is also often an economical one.

Frank Lloyd Wright's Fallingwater House, built between 1934 and 1937, is widely regarded as one of America's greatest works of architecture. The most prominent features of Wright's design are the reinforced concrete cantilever balconies projecting in 3 directions. Like Maillart, Wright achieved sincerity of form by leaving the concrete surfaces exposed. Unfortunately, he used far too little steel reinforcement, and the cantilevers began to sag almost immediately after the formwork was removed in 1937. In 2002, the building's caretakers initiated emergency structural repairs via the addition of high-strength steel cables, or tendons, to the cantilever beams—a process called **post tensioning**. This technique has been used in repair and construction of many reinforced concrete structures.

The most dramatic demonstration of concrete's versatility is its new role as the material of choice for the world's tallest buildings. In 1998, the Petronas Towers in Malaysia became the first concrete structure to claim the world's tallest building title; as of 2009, the reinforced concrete Burj Khalifa in Dubai held the title. The Burj Khalifa represents a revolutionary new generation of skyscraper technology; its buttressed core structural system is fundamentally different from any previous tall building. It consists of a series of medieval buttresses made of concrete but configured like steel I-beams, surmounted by a modernized version of the Eiffel Tower, demonstrating that sometimes engineering innovations are just old technologies applied in new ways, using new materials. ■

Important Terms

post tensioning: A system in which high-strength steel cables are threaded through holes or ducts in a precast concrete element, then tensioned with a hydraulic jack and anchored at their ends.

reinforced concrete: Concrete strengthened with iron or steel bars in regions subjected to tensile stress.

Suggested Reading

Addis, *Building*, chaps. 6–8.

Billington, *The Tower and the Bridge*, chaps. 9 and 11.

Nilson, Darwin, and Dolan, *Design of Concrete Structures*, chaps. 2, 3, and 19.

Questions to Consider

1. What is the relationship between form, function, and structure in the Ingalls Building?*

2. On the beam shown below, sketch the locations where steel reinforcement would be required.*

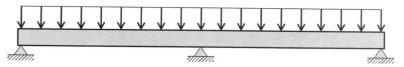

3. In what ways does the Salginatobel Bridge reflect the unique versatility of reinforced concrete?

4. How does post tensioning overcome the inherent limitations of concrete in beams?*

5. What aspects of the bridge below reflect the unique qualities of reinforced concrete?*

© iStockphoto/Thinkstock.

Amazing Thin Shells—Strength from Curvature
Lecture 21

You may think of the eggshell as the epitome of fragility, but in practice, it's actually astonishingly strong when it's subjected to a uniform loading. If I press on the egg from all directions, in compression it's capable of carrying a tremendous amount of load, in very much the same way that a shell-shaped roof would experience uniform loading.

The concrete parabolic arch that forms the front of Felix Candela's 1958 Chapel Lomas de Cuernavaca, Mexico, spans over 100 ft and is nearly 70 ft tall, yet only 1.5 in thick. It's a thin shell, a structural element that attains both strength and stiffness primarily from its curvature. Thin-shell structures can be made of just about any material, including wood, masonry, steel, and plastic. But since the 1920s, the finest thin shells have been made of our versatile friend, concrete.

The 19th-century mathematician Karl Gauss proved that any curved surface can be characterized as only 1 of 3 possible shapes: cylinder-like, dome-like, or saddle-like. All of these geometric shapes can be used as the basis for thin-shell structures. Cylinder-like shapes have curvature in only one direction. Dome-like shapes have curvature in both x and y directions, and both curvatures are oriented the same way. A saddle-like shape has curvature in both x and y directions, but one is concave up and the other is concave down. The dome-like and cylinder-like shapes we've seen in earlier lectures are quite thick; stiffness created by the opposing curvatures of the saddle shape is the unique advantage that allows saddle-shaped structures to be so thin.

Geometrically, a saddle shape is a parabolic shape extended along a parabolic path. The intersection of the 3-dimensional parabolic shape with a horizontal plane forms a hyperbola; thus we call such shapes hyperbolic paraboloids, or hypars. The hypar is particularly well suited for roofs not only because of its thickness but also because it can actually be generated with a series of straight lines, radiating diagonally from one parabolic end to the other.

A hypar carries load primarily in compression and works much like an arch. Downward loads are transmitted in compression out to the supports. The hypar can experience a little tension in the opposite direction, acting somewhat like a cable. Because they are so thin, hypar shells experience little or no bending stress.

The precursor of modern thin-shell structures is the dome of St. Paul's Cathedral in London, built between 1675 and 1710. Designed by one of England's greatest architects, Christopher Wren, with the assistance of mathematician Robert Hooke, it took advantage of Hooke's previous discovery that the catenary is the most structurally efficient shape for an arch. The dome is actually constructed in 3 layers: a cone-shaped brick shell supporting the 1000-ton stone lantern above; a thin, hemispherical, brick inner shell carrying only its own weight; and an outer dome made of lead-cover timber, protecting the cone from the elements and giving the structure the classic curved dome shape. The dome's thickness-to-span ratio is 1 to 37, versus 1 to 21 for Brunelleschi's dome and 1 to 11 for the Pantheon. Wren and Hooke had grasped the benefit and the possibilities of thinness.

The next major development in thin-shell structures was the timbrel vault. This traditional medieval Spanish masonry technique was modernized and brought to the U.S. in 1881 by Rafael

The ancient dome of the Pantheon works on precisely the same principles as today's thin-shell concrete domes.

Guastavino. Though they look like heavy stone masonry, Guastavino vaults are composed of several layers of ceramic tile, each less than an inch thick. These layered shells were used to create long-span roofs and intricate vaults of great strength and lightness, using no temporary formwork whatsoever. The thickness-to-span ratio of these shells was typically around 1 to 50.

Examples of Guastavino-style thin shells include the Boston Public Library, the Oyster Bar in New York's Grand Central Station, the Neo-Gothic vaulting of the Cadet Chapel at West Point, and the Great Hall at Ellis Island.

In the 1920s, the great revolution in thin-shell structures began in Germany when the Zeiss Corporation needed to construct a perfectly hemispherical interior surface for a planetarium out of flat facets. The surface also needed to be extremely light because it was to be built on top of an existing roof not designed to support an additional structural load. The dome's engineer, Walter Bauersfeld, based his design on the radiolarian sponge, which is a perfect sphere composed of 20 hexagons and 12 pentagons; a modern soccer ball uses the same configuration. The final product was a frame made of 3480 steel rods covered by spraying concrete onto a wire mesh backed up by a movable form. It has a thickness ratio of 1 to 130, the same as an eggshell. The Zeiss planetarium was the world's first true geodesic dome. Bauersfeld and his partners refined their system and went into business building thin-shell structures all over Europe, influencing designers there and around the world.

In 1935, Eduardo Torroja created one of the earliest major hypar concrete shell structures: the concrete canopy at the Madrid Hippodrome. These cantilever shells span over 40 ft; each is 5 in thick at its base and 2 in thick at its outer edge. During the Spanish Civil War, a bombardment punched numerous holes through these shells, but the structure stood firm.

Italian engineer Pier Luigi Nervi invented a technique using thin layers of concrete and wire mesh to create modular elements, which were then assembled using cast-in-place concrete connections. Nervi called his new composite material *ferrocemento*. His ribbed dome for the Palazzo dello Sport in Rome is a 330-ft-diameter shell assembled from V-shaped *ferrocemento* modules less than 1 in thick. Nervi even built sailboats and motorboats from *ferrocemento*.

The Sydney Opera House, designed by Danish architect Jørn Utzon, looks like a shell but is really a frame. A true thin shell is a continuum, a single structural component. Because of the expected wind loads on this building, Utzon had to construct his faux shell from 2400 discrete precast concrete ribs thick enough to resist bending. These ribs support 4000 individual concrete panels. The Auditorio de Tenerife in the Canary Islands, designed by Santiago Calatrava, is aesthetically similar to the Sydney Opera House but is a true shell, specifically a cantilever hypar shell. In this, as in all such structures, aesthetic beauty and structural strength derive from exactly the same source: the curved shape of the shell. ■

Important Terms

ferrocemento: A construction technique that used thin layers of concrete and wire mesh to create modular elements, which were then assembled by using cast-in-place concrete connections. *Ferrocemento* was developed by Pier Luigi Nervi.

hyperbolic paraboloid (a.k.a. **hypar**): A saddle-like shape.

thin shell: A structural element that attains both strength and stability from its curved shape.

timbrel vault: A thin-shell vault made of multiple layers of ceramic tile.

Suggested Reading

Addis, *Building*, chaps. 4, 8, and 9.

Billington, *The Tower and the Bridge*, chap. 10.

Salvadori, *Why Buildings Stand Up*, chap. 11.

Questions to Consider

1. What is the relationship between form, function, and structure in the dome of St. Paul's Cathedral? In Chapel Lomas de Cuernavaca?*

2. What are the structural advantages of a timbrel vault versus traditional masonry vaulting?*

3. Given their beauty and economical use of materials, why do you think thin shells are not more widely used in modern construction? Why have thin shells been more popular in Mexico than in the United States?*

4. What does the case of the Sydney Opera House tell us about the limitations of thin-shell structures?*

Vast Roof Systems of Iron and Steel
Lecture 22

Successful long-span structural configurations don't ever seem to go away. They evolve; they're refined; sometimes they fall out of fashion for a period and then they're rediscovered; but as it turns out, many groundbreaking long-span structural configurations of the 19ᵗʰ century are still used in some of our most modern structures today.

The historical transition from masonry to iron-framed domes closely parallels the transition from solid masonry walls to iron-framed structural systems in buildings, and it happened for many of the same reasons: reduced weight, greater strength, and larger windows. The world's first long-span iron roof was the dome of the Paris Grain Market, designed in 1802. This 128-ft-diameter hemisphere was an iron grid sheathed in copper. The semicircular cast-iron meridian arches carried load in compression and the wrought-iron parallels carried load in tension, echoing the lines of tension and compression in masonry domes. The dome weighs 34 lbs/ft² of covered floor area, versus Brunelleschi's brick cathedral dome at 700 lbs/ft².

Compare the Houston Astrodome, a modern framed dome constructed in 1965. At 642 ft in diameter and 208 ft above the playing field, the dome is a thin slice of a sphere—the same shallow spherical configuration used to minimize hoop stresses in Hagia Sophia's dome. Unlike the masonry dome at Hagia Sophia, the steel Astrodome's strong lateral thrust is easily handled through a tension ring at the base. The frame was designed not only to carry its own weight but also to withstand hurricane-force winds. Functionally, the frame behaves exactly like the frame of the Paris Grain Market dome. Although the Houston Astrodome was the world's first domed stadium, it employed no new technologies or major structural concepts.

The early railroad stations of the Industrial Revolution are sometimes called the cathedrals of the 19ᵗʰ century—public spaces that reflected the technological prowess of the era. The original roof over the passenger platforms at London's Euston Station, built in 1837, was supported on short iron trusses. The roof of the train shed of St. Pancras Station, built 30 years later, was built on 100-ft-tall trussed arches, similar to its contemporaries, the Eads Bridge and the Garabit Viaduct. Today, the train shed is part of the Eurostar passenger terminal. Europe's largest and most modern train station is the Berlin Hauptbahnhof. The principal structural element of the vaulted roof of the east-west train hall is a lightweight arch with a flat profile that the designers call a basket-handle arch. The arches are reinforced with lightweight trusses—1 internal and 2 external—to offset the tendency of a shallow arch to flatten under load.

Until the end of the 18th century, virtually all iron and steel trusses were 2-dimensional; engineers didn't have methods to analyze more complex structural geometries. In the 1930s, German engineer Max Mengeringhausen began experimenting with 3-dimensional truss configurations called **space trusses**. He created the MERO construction system, consisting of mass-produced steel rods and connector nodes with threaded holes, allowing up to 18 members to connect from different directions. Mengeringhausen's company, now called MERO Structures, recently built an immense space truss for the national performing arts center of Singapore. It's hard to believe that this ultramodern design uses technology from the 1930s.

Because the engineers were schooled in traditional 2-dimensional analysis, they weren't able to visualize the 3-dimensional behavior of this unique structure.

With the success of the MERO system and the advent of computer-based structural analysis methods, space trusses became increasingly popular. The roof of the Hartford Civic Center was a MERO-built single space truss: a rectangular grid of 120 interconnected modules, each shaped like an inverted pyramid, producing a light, delicate roof that appeared to float in midair. The concrete roof deck above the trusses was supported on vertical posts extending from the joints connecting the trusses' top chords, rather than resting directly on the trusses. This turned out to be a crucial error: The roof collapsed in a moderate snowstorm only a few years after construction. The main cause of the failure was inadequate lateral bracing of the top truss chords at the roof's perimeter. Had the roof lain directly on the trusses, it would have braced the chords, and the structure would not have collapsed. Because the engineers were schooled in traditional 2-dimensional analysis, they weren't able to visualize the 3-dimensional behavior of this unique structure.

Few modern long-span structures are more impressive than the University of Phoenix Stadium's retractable roof, built in 2006. It is as large as the playing field and retracts lengthwise. Two immense steel **lenticular trusses** run the 700-ft length of the stadium, supporting the outer edges of the roof. The curved bottom chord is made of 2 heavy steel I-shaped members, but it functions like a draped cable in tension; the curved top chord—a 3-dimensional truss in its own right—works like an arch in compression. The compression and tension counterbalance each other, so the structure generates no lateral thrust at its supports. The trusses have essentially the same shape as the parabolic moment diagram of a simply supported beam, which makes sense because sometimes trusses carry load just like beams do.

The University of Phoenix Stadium roof is a highly sophisticated reflection of modern structural engineering know-how, and yet its configuration is nearly identical to the main trusses of the Royal Albert Bridge at Saltash, England, built in 1859 by Isambard Kingdom Brunel. That's why Walter P. Moore, the structural engineer of record for the Phoenix Stadium roof, named his trusses "Brunel trusses." They are a perfect example of both continuity and innovation. ∎

Important Terms

lenticular truss: A lens-shaped truss.

space truss: A truss with a geometric configuration that can only be defined in 3-dimensional space, rather than a 2-dimensional plane.

velarium: A fabric awning that was stretched over the seating area of the Roman Colosseum to shade the spectators.

Suggested Reading

Addis, *Building*, chaps. 6, 7, and 9.

Billington, *The Tower and the Bridge*, chap. 3.

Salvadori and Levy, *Why Buildings Fall Down*, chap. 4.

Questions to Consider

1. How were the designs of the Paris Grain Market and the Houston Astrodome influenced by the available materials—cast and wrought iron for the Grain Market, steel for the Astrodome?*

2. How is science-based design reflected in the configuration of the Berlin Hauptbahnhof?*

3. What does the Hartford Civic Center collapse tell us about the challenges inherent in the design of innovative structures?

4. Why has the development of new sports complexes provided such a strong stimulus for structural engineering innovation in recent years?

The Incredible Lightness of Tension Structures
Lecture 23

In 1968, the roof of Madison Square Garden was regarded as an innovative structure; nonetheless, in terms of load carrying, it is identical to the ancient velarium, that rope-and-canvas awning over the Coliseum in Rome. ... The Garden's suspended dish roof protects today's fans of sport and spectacle as they enjoy the modern equivalent of gladiatorial combat.

A s a general rule, a tension member can be significantly lighter and more slender than a compression member, even if the magnitude of the internal force is the same in both cases, because compression members buckle and tension members don't. In Brunel's Royal Albert Bridge, for example, the magnitude of the compression force in the truss's top chords is about the same as the magnitude of the tension force in the bottom chords, yet the top chords are huge iron tubes, while the bottom chords are light eyebar chains. Therefore structures in which all of the principal load-carrying elements are in tension are exceptionally light and efficient.

Tension structures are usually composed of steel cables, sometimes integrated with a thin, flexible, synthetic fabric membrane. They are distinctly modern structural configurations, although there is one ancient antecedent: the Roman Colosseum's rope-and-canvas awning—the velarium. A structural element can carry tension in only one way: through internal force directed along its axis. Therefore, load paths are very evident in tension structures, and the principle of equilibrium is often beautifully illustrated at the joints.

The world's first cable-supported roof was the 1952 J. S. Dorton Arena in Raleigh, North Carolina. The roof is suspended from 2 intersecting, parabolic, reinforced concrete arches. A set of cables runs from arch to arch, while a second set runs across each arch. The cables are topped by lightweight steel-clad sheeting. While this resembles the shape of a hypar shell, it carries the load in tension, whereas a shell carries load in compression. Interestingly, while the arches obviously support the roof, the roof also supports the arches;

the cables actually help to hold them up. And while the roof is a tension structure, other structural elements of the building are in compression. We'll see this characteristic in all the tension structures in this lecture.

The David S. Ingalls Hockey Rink at Yale University, built in 1958 by Eero Saarinen and Fred Severud, has a completely different physical appearance but uses a similar structural concept. Its curved central spine is a reinforced concrete arch nearly 300 ft long. Steel cables run from the top of the arch outward in both directions and are anchored at the tops of the building's curved walls. The inward pull of these cables is counterbalanced by the curved walls, acting very much like arches turned sideways. The steel cables then support a timber roof, and the weight of that roof gives the cables their curved shape.

Severud is also responsible for New York City's Madison Square Garden, constructed in 1968. The Garden's 425-ft-diameter cylindrical outer shell is a steel frame with precast concrete walls, but the roof is a tension structure called a hanging dish, which consists of 2 concentric steel rings, the outer supported by columns and the inner suspended on a series of cables running between the rings. The whole is topped with precast concrete panels supported on the cables.

This roof beautifully illustrates equilibrium in action: the cables, in tension, pull outward on the central ring, which is therefore also in tension. Meanwhile, the cables also pull inward on the outer ring, which is therefore a compression ring. There is no net outward thrust or inward pull transmitted by the roof system to the structural system below, only the downward weight of the roof. From an engineering perspective, the hanging dish is the direct opposite of a dome: Each cable is a catenary, the base ring is in compression rather than tension, and the central ring is in tension rather than compression.

A "bicycle wheel" variation on the hanging dish roof was constructed for the Utica Memorial Auditorium in upstate New York in the late 1950s. The cables are run in pairs separated by vertical struts. Unlike the Garden's roof, which needs a special drainage system, this roof slopes outward, an essential feature in a snow-prone cold climate. It is also stiffer than a simple hanging dish, improving its resistance to wind-induced vibrations.

In the early 1950s, a young German architecture student named Frei Otto visited Fred Severud's office while Severud was working on the Dorton Arena. Inspired by what he saw, Otto returned to Germany and began designing cable-net and membrane structures. He defined his shapes not with mathematical models but with physical ones made of chain, string, netting, plastic sheets, and even soap bubbles in some cases. This so-called form-finding method—reminiscent of Gaudi's technique for La Sagrada Familia—has produced unique structures like the 1972 Olympiapark in Munich, a series of cable-reinforced polyester fabric membranes stretched between cable-stayed columns. Since the 1980s, high-powered computer models have allowed engineers and architects to accomplish this same end computationally, but Otto's natural forms still serve as the inspiration for many modern tension structures. ■

Important Terms

membrane: A synthetic fabric used as a structural element in a tension structure.

tension structure: A structural system in which most of the principal load-carrying elements are cables or membranes carrying load in tension.

Suggested Reading

Addis, *Building*, chap. 9.

Buchholdt, *Introduction to Cable Roof Structures*, chap. 1.

Salvadori, *Why Buildings Stand Up*, chap. 16.

Questions to Consider

1. In what ways is the roof of the J. S. Dorton Arena similar to the roof of Chapel Lomas de Cuernavaca? In what ways are they different?*

2. In what ways is the hanging dish roof system similar to a dome? In what ways is it different?*

3. Describe how a bicycle wheel functions as a tension structure. In what ways is the bicycle-wheel roof system of the Utica Auditorium similar to an actual bicycle wheel? In what ways is it different?*

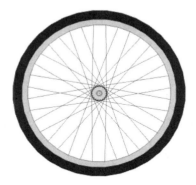

4. The photo below is the Kurilpa Bridge in Brisbane, Australia—the world's largest tensegrity bridge. Can you explain how the structural system carries load? In what ways is it similar to David Geiger's cable dome at the Seoul Gymnastics Hall? In what ways is it different?*

Strategies for Understanding Any Structure
Lecture 24

Now that you've learned all the major principles of structural mechanics and examined many of the world's greatest structures in terms of those principles, you should be able to analyze any structure you come across—great or humble—just as we have in this course. In this lecture, you have the chance to test your newfound analytical skills as we look at one last group of great structures.

Perhaps the most straightforward approach to understanding a new structure is by direct comparison with structures you've already seen. For example, the dome of the U.S. Capitol can be understood through direct comparison with the dome of St. Paul's Cathedral in London. Like Saint Paul's, the Capitol dome uses a 3-part configuration: nonstructural outer and inner shells concealing a parabolic structural dome. Both work the same way; the only significant difference is that St. Paul's structural dome is brick, while the Capitol's structural dome is an open iron framework. In this difference, we can see the influence of the iron-framed dome of the Paris Grain Market, built about 100 years after St. Paul's and about 50 years before the Capitol.

Similarly, when we encounter the spectacular new Tokyo Sky Tree, we should recognize it as a descendant of the Eiffel Tower. The Sky Tree, at 2080 ft, is the world's tallest tower. Its overall shape and truss construction reflect the same response to wind load that Eiffel used in Paris, but the Sky Tree goes further, with a reinforced concrete core and a uniquely varying cross-section: triangular at the base, for stability, transitioning to circular at the top, for decreased wind resistance.

But what happens when you encounter structures in unfamiliar categories? Perhaps you can draw analogies with different types of structures that nonetheless carry load in the same way. For example, we haven't discussed dams in this course, yet you can see at a glance that the Hoover Dam is just an arch turned sideways, holding back a wall of water the same way that the Pont-Saint-Martin's arch carries the weight of the stone above it. The Chunnel linking England and France beneath the English Channel is also a variation on the arch. Consisting of 2 rail tunnels and 1 service tunnel, it is lined with arc-shaped precast concrete segments that, on examination, closely resemble voissoirs—only in this case the shape they create is a full circle instead of a hemisphere or parabola. Also, like the corbelled dome of the Treasury of Atreus, its members are held in place by soil pressure.

Sometimes you'll encounter a structure that superficially resembles one of our categories but is actually something else entirely. For example, the Qiancheng Bridge in China's Fujian Province is a rainbow bridge, a style that dates to the 11th century A.D. It is not an arch; there's no lateral support at its base. In fact, it's a rigid frame that gets its rigidity from this interweaving of transverse and longitudinal elements. Its members carry load in bending and axial compression combined, rather than in compression like an arch. One

The Hoover Dam is an arch turned on its side. It carries the horizontal weight of water the same way an arch bridge carries vertical load.

example of a modern frame bridge is the Fahy Bridge over the Lehigh River in Bethlehem, Pennsylvania.

When you encounter a structure for which there aren't any obvious analogies, you can return to the technique of analyzing the structural system we discussed in Lecture 9. The Strömsund Bridge in Sweden, built in 1956, is considered the first modern cable-stayed bridge. Cable-stayed bridges are often confused with suspension bridges, but they are entirely different. Their horizontal equilibrium requires the main girder to resist compression as well as bending, so it must be much more substantial than the stiffening girder of a suspension bridge. Also, unlike in a suspension bridge, the cables of a cable-stayed bridge are always perfectly straight; therefore, a large concentrated load in the center span of the bridge can cause a tendency to either bend or overturn the towers. Attaching the outermost stay cables, called back stays, to the girder near the concrete abutments counterbalances the overturning tendency with a downward reaction at the abutment.

The Strömsund Bridge is a conventional cable-stayed configuration, but many more recent variations include, for example, different numbers of towers, requiring different tower shapes to offset the overturning tendency. For example, the Alamillo Bridge in Seville, Spain, designed by Santiago Calatrava and constructed in 1992, has a single tower with no backstays at all. The backward lean of the tower counterbalances the tendency of the tension in the cable stays to rotate the tower forward, toward the center span. Compare Calatrava's Samuel Beckett Bridge in Dublin, Ireland. The forward-leaning tower—designed to resemble a harp, the national symbol of Ireland—required an inward-leaning tower and 2 very substantial backstays to stabilize it. Note that in all of these examples, the distinguishing characteristics of the structures can be understood in terms of a single concept: the equilibrium of the tower against overturning. Thus a qualitative structural system analysis can open the door to a deep understanding of an entire category of structure.

That said, you can gain many fascinating and rewarding insights about structures without any sort of formal analysis. Structures often communicate with us in clear and compelling ways simply through the shapes and proportions of their elements. The 12 towers of London's Millennium Dome tell us that they carry load in compression by their stout proportions and the orientations of the attached stay-cables. The array of cables radiating out from the towers tells us that they carry tension by virtue of their slender proportions. We might call this the language of structure.

Let's conclude this course with a look at my personal favorite structure, Pier Nervi's Palazzetto dello Sport in Rome, built in 1957—not to be confused with Nervi's Palazzo dello Sport from Lecture 21. The Palazzetto is smaller and even more interesting as a structural system. The thin-shell dome was built from hundreds of individual diamond-shaped *ferrocemento* shells. These modules were positioned on scaffolding and connected by pouring a thin layer of concrete on top, producing a structure of extraordinary strength and lightness—and beauty. In a way, it evokes the ancient dome of the Pantheon; the ferrocemento diamonds fulfill the same role as the Pantheon's coffers, and the dome incorporates an oculus as well.

> **You can gain many fascinating and rewarding insights about structures without any sort of formal analysis.**

Near the base of the dome, the pattern in the concrete ribs changes to channel compressive forces out into discrete points of support at its bottom edge, just as the pendentives of Hagia Sophia channel the weight of the dome into the supporting columns. On the exterior of the Palazzetto, these points of support connect to flying buttresses like those on a Gothic cathedral, but Nervi's buttresses are triangulated, so they also function as trusses to stabilize the dome against lateral loads. Finally, the foundation serves as a tension ring, which contains the lateral thrust of the buttresses in much the same way that Filippo Brunelleschi's stone chains contained the thrust of his dome over the cathedral of Santa Maria del Fiore in Florence. This structure is an amazing combination of elements drawing on the technologies of ancient Rome, Byzantium, medieval Europe, and Renaissance Italy, yet combined in a way that's thoroughly modern, beautifully integrated, and perfectly expressive of structural purpose. ■

Addis, *Building*, chap. 8.

Billington, *The Tower and the Bridge*.

Salvadori, *Why Buildings Stand Up*, chap. 17.

Tzonis, *Santiago Calatrava*.

Questions to Consider

1. What is the relationship between form, function, and structure in the Hoover Dam?*

2. How are cable-stayed bridges similar to suspension bridges? How are they different?*

3. Think of a building, bridge, or tower that you would like to learn more about. Which of the following strategies (discussed in Lecture 24) might you use to increase your understanding of this structure?

   • Compare it with similar structures covered in this course.

   • Look for analogies with different types of structures that carry load in essentially the same way.

   • Analyze the structural system.

   • Consider the relationship between form, function, and structure.

   • Read the language of structure—determine how structural elements carry load simply through their shapes and proportions.

Answers to Selected Questions

Lecture 2

1. The free-body diagram of the diving board is shown below. *A* and *B* are reactions at the points where the board is attached to its supports. *W* is the weight of the diver. The only way this body can be in equilibrium is for the reaction *A* to be oriented downward and *B* to be oriented upward. Otherwise, the board would be subjected to an unbalanced moment.

2. To solve the equilibrium problem, first draw a free-body diagram of the bridge. As shown below, the diagram should include both the 5-lb live load and the 2-lb self-weight, as well as the unknown reactions R_L and R_R.

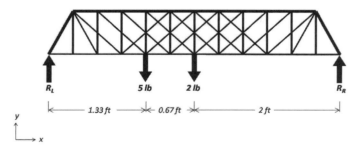

Now write the equations of equilibrium. There are no forces in the x direction, so the equation $\Sigma F_x = 0$ is not relevant. The other 2 equations are as follows:

$$\sum F_y = 0$$

$R_L + R_R - 5 \text{ lb} - 2 \text{ lb} = 0$

$R_L + R_R = 7 \text{ lb}$

$$\sum M_L = 0$$

(5 lb) (1.33 ft) + (2 lb) (2 ft) - R$_R$ (4 ft) = 0

R$_R$ (4 ft) = 10.65 ft lb

R$_R$ = 2.66 lb

Now substitute this result into the previous equation to solve for R_L.

$R_L + 2.66 \text{ lb} = 7 \text{ lb}$

$R_L = 4.34 \text{ lb}$

Therefore, the reactions at the left and right ends of the bridge are 4.34 lb and 2.66 lb, respectively. Do these answers make sense? Yes, because the 5-lb load is shifted toward the left end of the bridge, it makes sense that the left reaction is larger.

3. When you stand on 2 feet, the free-body diagram of your body has 3 forces—your weight (W), applied at your center of gravity, and 2 reactions (L and R) pushing upward on your feet, as shown below. The lengths x_L and x_R are the horizontal distances from the reactions to your center of gravity. When you are standing erect, x_L and x_R are equal. If you lean to the left, as shown below, x_L gets smaller and x_R gets larger.

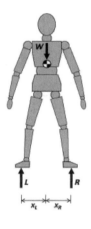 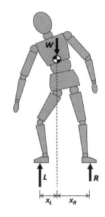

The equilibrium equations corresponding to this free body diagram are as follows:

$$\sum F_y = 0$$

$$L + R - W = 0$$

$$L + R = W$$

$$\sum M_R = 0$$

$$L(x_L + x_R) - Wx_R = 0$$

$$L(x_L + x_R) - Wx_R = 0$$

$$L = \frac{Wx_R}{x_L + x_R}$$

These equations tell us that, as x_R gets larger, L gets larger and R gets smaller. Physically, as you lean to the left, more of your weight is carried on your left foot and less on your right foot. You can safely continue to lean until your center of gravity is directly over 1 ft. When your center of gravity is directly over your left foot, $W = L$ and $R = 0$. At this point, your body is still in equilibrium, but if you lean just a bit farther, you will fall over. Mathematically, this condition corresponds to a reversal in the direction of the reaction R (from upward to downward). This reversal is not physically possible unless your feet are glued to the floor. If they are not, then your body can no longer remain in equilibrium, and it tips over. Therefore, when you stand on 2 feet, you can lean a considerable distance in either direction without falling over. The farther apart your feet are, the more you can lean without becoming unstable. When you are standing on only 1 foot, as shown below, the free-body diagram has only 2 forces. The only way this system can be in equilibrium is for your center of gravity to be located directly above the reaction R, as shown in the diagram at left. When you balance on 1 foot, you are instinctively adjusting the position of your center of gravity to achieve this equilibrium position. If you lean just a little bit, as shown below at right, the forces W and R cause an unbalanced moment. The unbalanced moment causes you to tip over. And that is why it is harder to stand on 1 foot than on 2.

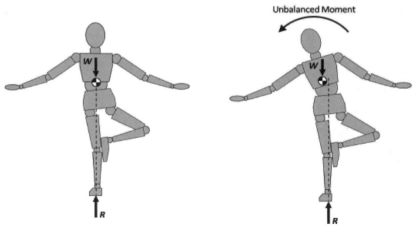

4. 4. At the left-hand end of the lifting arm is a counterweight, which balances the weight of the bridge deck. Thus very little additional force is required to rotate the lifting arm.

Lecture 3

1. Stress is defined as the internal force divided by the cross-sectional area. Thus, the stress can be reduced by reducing the internal force or increasing the cross-sectional area of the member.

2. Strain is defined as the deformation divided by the original length. If the strain is equal to 1.0, then the deformation is equal to the original length. In other words, the length of the member has doubled.

3. *Material A* has the highest stress-strain curve, so it is the strongest. *Material B* has the steepest slope in the elastic region of the stress-strain curve, so it is stiffest. *Material C* has the largest strain at fracture (i.e., the longest stress-strain curve), so it is the most ductile.

4. The slender cables radiating out from the top of the tower are all tension members.

Lecture 4

1. Wood is the most commonly used structural material in U.S. residential construction because it is highly economical. Wood can be cut and assembled without specialized tools or equipment and without many of the high-skill workers (e.g., welders, steel fabricators, crane operators, masons) required for heavy construction. U.S. building codes specify standardized systems for determining member sizes and configurations, so most residential wood-frame construction can be accomplished without employing a professional engineer. The economy of wood-frame construction is further enhanced by the availability of a wide variety of compatible building components—doors, windows, electrical fixtures, and plumbing fixtures.

2. Concrete is the world's most common construction material because of its durability, versatility of form, and wide availability. Concrete is made of cement, aggregates, and water. Aggregates and water are inexpensive and available in most parts of the world—often in close proximity to construction sites. Portland cement is manufactured in many regions and can be easily shipped throughout the world. Concrete can be mixed and placed with simple tools and equipment.

3. Both concrete and cast iron are shaped by pouring the material in a liquid state into a mold. Both materials are relatively strong in compression and weak in tension.

4. Many modern materials have engineering properties that would make them quite useful in structural applications; however, in general, these materials are significantly more expensive than steel. Many of these modern materials also lack the steel's ductility and its capacity to be connected by welding.

Lecture 5

1. The compression member is likely to be significantly heavier because it must be designed to resist buckling and material failure. A tension member is not susceptible to buckling, so its design only must account for material failure.

2. The free-body diagram of Trajan's Column is shown at right. Its weight is W; its height is h; and the reaction at its base is designated as R. We begin with the definition stress = F/A, where F is the internal force and A is the cross-sectional area. In this column, the maximum internal force occurs at the base and is exactly equal to the weight W. By definition, $W = V\gamma$, where V is the volume and γ is the density of the material. If we assume that the column is a cylinder, then the volume is $V = hA$. Putting the previous 3 equations together:

$$\text{stress} = \frac{F}{A} = \frac{W}{A} = \frac{V\gamma}{A} = \frac{hA\gamma}{A}$$

After simplifying this equation, we get stress = $h\gamma$. Therefore, the stress at the base of the column is simply the height h times the density of the material γ. Substituting the given values:

$$\text{stress} = (112 \text{ ft})\left(450 \frac{\text{lb}}{\text{ft}^3}\right) = 50{,}400 \frac{\text{lb}}{\text{ft}^2}$$

Now we can convert the answer to the more common units for stress, pounds per square inch:

$$\text{stress} = \left(50{,}400 \frac{\text{lb}}{\text{ft}^2}\right)\left(\frac{1 \text{ ft}^2}{144 \text{ in}^2}\right) = 350 \frac{\text{lb}}{\text{in}^2} = 350 \text{ psi}$$

For cast iron, the factor of safety is as follows:

$$\text{factor of safety} = \frac{\text{strength}}{\text{actual stress}} = \frac{80000 \text{ psi}}{350 \text{ psi}} = 229$$

In other words, if Trajan's Column were made of cast iron, its strength would be over 200 times greater than the actual stress caused by its own weight.

3. First calculate the force at which material failure occurs. The definition of stress is F/A, where F is the internal force and A is the cross-sectional area. At the point of material failure, stress = strength. We can combine these expressions to solve for the failure force:

$$\text{strength} = \frac{\text{failure force}}{A} \qquad\qquad \text{failure force} = (\text{strength})(A)$$

The cross-sectional area of a circular cross-section is πr^2. Substituting the given material strength and column radius:

$$\text{failure force} = (\text{strength})(\pi r^2) = \left(50{,}000 \; \frac{\text{lb}}{\text{in}^2}\right)(3.14159)(5 \; \text{in})^2$$

$$\text{failure force} = 3927000 \; \text{lb}$$

To calculate the force at which buckling occurs (also called the buckling strength), use the Euler buckling equation:

$$P_{\text{critical}} = \frac{\pi^2 EI}{L^2}$$

For a 10-inch diameter circular cross-section,

$$I = \frac{\pi r^4}{4} = \frac{\pi (5 \; \text{in})^4}{4} = 490.9 \; \text{in}^4$$

To draw a graph, we will need to calculate P_{critical} for a range of different column lengths. For $L = 20 \; \text{ft} = 240 \; \text{in}$, the calculation is as follows:

$$P_{\text{critical}} = \frac{\pi^2 EI}{L^2} = \frac{\pi^2 \left(29{,}000{,}000 \frac{\text{lb}}{\text{in}^2}\right)(490.9 \; \text{in}^4)}{(240 \; \text{in})^2} = 2{,}439{,}000 \; \text{lb}$$

For $L = 40 \; \text{ft} = 480 \; \text{in}$, the calculation is as follows:

$$P_{\text{critical}} = \frac{\pi^2 EI}{L^2} = \frac{\pi^2 \left(29{,}000{,}000 \frac{\text{lb}}{\text{in}^2}\right)(490.9 \; \text{in}^4)}{(480 \; \text{in})^2} = 610{,}000 \; \text{lb}$$

After repeating this calculation for other representative lengths (a task that is best performed with a spreadsheet), the graph of strength versus length can be plotted. The result is shown below. Note that, when the length is less than 190 in, buckling occurs at a higher force than material failure; thus, material failure controls the strength of short columns. Because material strength does not change with column length, the strength curve is horizontal when the length is less than 190 in.

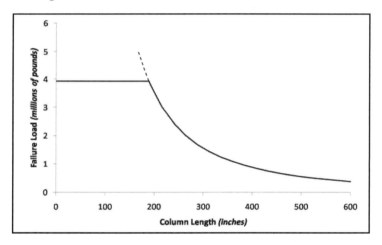

Lecture 6

1. The moment diagrams for the 2 beams are shown below. From these diagrams, we can see that the simply supported beam with 2 equal loads has its maximum internal moment in the middle of the span, between the 2 loads. The cantilever beam has its maximum internal moment at the supported end. Note also that the internal moment is positive in the simply supported beam and negative in the cantilever beam. This difference is reflected in the fact that the simply supported beam bends concave upward, while the cantilever bends concave downward.

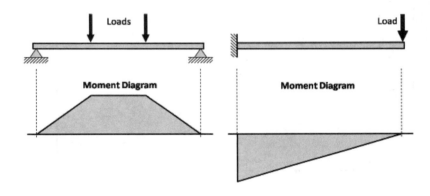

2. Stress in a beam can be reduced by decreasing the internal moment or increasing the area moment of inertia. The internal moment can be reduced by reducing the external loads or by adding additional supports. The area moment of inertia can be increased by making the beam cross-section larger or by changing its shape, such that more material is distributed farther away from the axis of the beam (for example, by using an I-shaped cross-section rather than a solid rectangular cross-section).

3. A simply supported beam is somewhat simpler to build than a continuous beam, so its construction cost may be lower. A simply supported beam is also better able to accommodate movement of its supports caused by settlement of the soil beneath the foundations. Finally, in some situations (e.g., a bridge spanning a deep valley), building the additional intermediate support required for a continuous beam might be impossible or prohibitively expensive.

4. The deflected shape and moment diagram of the beam are shown below. Between points A and C, the beam bends concave downward. Thus, in this region, it experiences tension on top and compression below. Between points C and E, the beam bends concave upward. Here, it experiences compression on top and tension below.

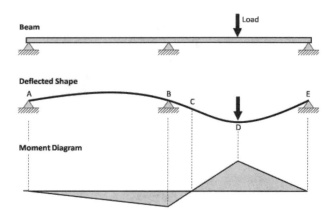

Lecture 7

1. Most trusses have one or more members that carry load in tension. Because stone and concrete have very low tensile strength, they are unsuitable for use in trusses.

2. One main truss of the bridge is annotated on the photograph below.

Photo Courtesy of Dr. Stephen Ressler.

The free-body diagram of this truss is shown below. Note that, because there are 2 main trusses, each one carries half of the weight of the 100,000-lb locomotive.

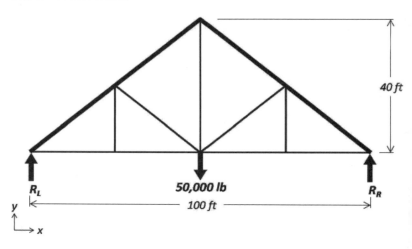

3. Before we can calculate internal forces, we must first determine the reactions R_L and R_R. In this case, both the structure and loads are symmetrical, and so the 2 reactions must be equal and must add up to 50,000 lb. Thus, $R_L = R_R = 25,000$ pounds. Now we isolate the joint at the lower left corner of the truss and draw a free-body diagram of it.

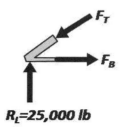

R_L=25,000 lb

The corresponding polygon of forces is shown below. Note that the three forces are arranged tip to tail, and each is oriented in the same direction as the corresponding force on the free-body diagram.

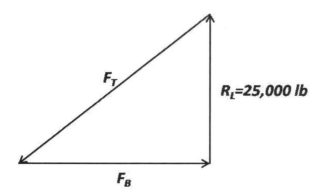

Now the 2 unknown forces can be determined from the geometry of the triangle. This problem can be solved using trigonometry, but to solve the problem graphically (as Squire Whipple might have done), measure all 3 sides of the triangle and then determine the scale of the drawing by relating the length of the vertical side to the magnitude of the corresponding force—25,000 lb. Finally, use this scale to determine the other 2 forces. For example, suppose the vertical line is 3-1/8 in long. This is the same as 25/8 in, so the scale is 1/8 in =1000 lb. Now we measure the diagonal line and find it to be 5 in long. This is the same as 40/8 in, so the corresponding force F_T is approximately equal to 40,000 lb. Using the same procedure, we can determine the force F_B to be approximately 31,000 lb. Based on the directions of the internal forces, as shown on the free-body diagram, the force in the bottom chord is in tension, and the force in the top chord is in compression. Thus the final result is F_B = 31,000 lb in tension and F_T = 40,000 lb in compression.

4. The top chord is a heavy box-shaped cross-section. Since this sort of configuration is required to resist buckling, the top chord must be in compression. The bottom chord is a thin bar, and the center vertical member is a pair of slender rods. Because these members are so slender, they would buckle at an extremely low level of compressive force; thus, they must be in tension. The proportions of the remaining diagonal and vertical members are somewhat ambiguous; thus, we would need to use the method of joints to determine whether they are in tension or compression under a given loading.

5. Each connection in the main truss consists of a single pin. This configuration identifies the structure as relatively old—most likely a 19th century or early 20th century structure. Squire Whipple published his science-based method of truss analysis in 1847. To facilitate mathematical analysis, this method assumes that all joints are pins. In the succeeding decades, most engineers designed trusses with single-pin connections, to conform with the underlying assumption of the analysis method. By contrast, the Eiffel Tower made use of gusset-plate connections in 1889, and during the early 20th century, gusset-plate connections gradually replaced pinned connections. Gusset-plate connections are safer because of their greater redundancy, but they are more analytically complex. This particular bridge, called a Waddell A Truss, was constructed in 1898.

Lecture 8

1. As shown in the lecture, the principle of equilibrium can be used to develop an equation for the tension, T, at mid-span in a cable subjected to a horizontally distributed load. The result is

$$T = \frac{(\text{load})(\text{span})^2}{8(\text{sag})}$$

The Golden Gate Bridge has 2 main cables, and we can reasonably assume that each cable carries half of the total load. Substituting the given dimensions and the load of 10,000 lb/ft,

$$T = \frac{(10000\frac{\text{lb}}{\text{ft}})(4200 \text{ ft})^2}{8(500 \text{ ft})} = 44,100,000 \text{ lb}$$

Thus each cable carries approximately 44 million pounds (22,000 tons) at mid-span.

2. A free body diagram of the structure is shown below.

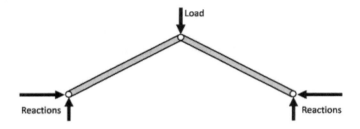

This structure carries load as an arch, because it generates both vertical and horizontal reactions at its supports and because both of its structural elements are in compression.

3. Although we cannot know the specific reasons why the designers chose these 2 different configurations, we can make a few relevant observations:

   • The bridge in the foreground is made of steel, while the bridge in the background is concrete. The first bridge has a longer span and a flatter profile—conditions that cause greater compression in the arch and greater lateral thrust. Thus the designer's decision to use the stronger material (steel) would have enabled the use of a more demanding structural configuration.

   • The bridge in the background has a higher roadway elevation, which would have required taller arches.

   • The bridge in the foreground spans the full width of the river, while the bridge in the background uses an intermediate pier in the channel. It is possible that conditions on the riverbed did not favor the construction of a pier at the location of the first bridge or that the cost of constructing such a pier was judged to be too high.

Lecture 9

1. The maximum snow load on a bridge would correspond to an extremely large snowfall. The maximum traffic load would correspond to bumper-to-bumper traffic extending along the full length of the bridge. It is extremely unlikely that both of these situations would occur simultaneously. When a large snowfall occurs, traffic is usually diminished. Thus, bridges are generally not designed to carry maximum snow load and maximum traffic load simultaneously.

2. The principal load applied to the structure is the weight of people sitting on the bench. The bench carries these loads as a beam, supported by a pair of chains at each end. These chains are tension members, which

transmit the weight of the people and bench up to the horizontal ridge beam at the top of the structure. This member carries load in flexure and is supported at the tops of 2 A-frames. The 2 frames transmit the accumulated weight of the entire structural system down to 4 concrete footings. The triangular shape of the frames is also particularly effective in resisting front-to-back forces generated when the swing is in motion. The 2 diagonal braces connecting the A-frames to the ridge beam provide lateral stability: they prevent the structure from tipping over sideways.

Lecture 10

1. The function of the Treasury of Atreus was to provide a tomb, possibly for an important sovereign of Mycenae. This function dictated the monumental size and high-quality construction of the tomb. The form of the Treasury of Atreus features a circular plan and a roughly conical profile, completely covered over with soil. Every aspect of this form derives directly from the structure of the Treasury of Atreus—a corbelled dome. The circular plan is essential for the stability of a corbelled dome. The roughly conical profile is also characteristic of this structural configuration, with progressively smaller rings of stone placed at progressively higher levels. The underground location was dictated by the need to use compacted earth to stabilize the dome from the outside. Thus, form follows structure in the Treasury of Atreus.

2. A true arch is composed of wedge-shaped voussoirs that carry load in compression. The arch as a whole can carry load only if lateral support is provided at its base. A corbelled arch is composed of horizontal layers of stone, each successive layer extending inward slightly from the previous layer on either side of the arch opening. Thus the end stone in each layer is a cantilever beam, which carries load in flexure. The corbelled arch does not require lateral support at its base for stability, but it does require layers of masonry above the cantilevered stones to counterbalance them.

Lecture 11

1. The principal function of this building was to enclose a cold-water bath. The entire facility also had an important symbolic function—communicating the power of Rome and the benevolence of the Emperor Caracalla. To accomplish these functions, the form of the building was a vast interior space, amply illuminated with natural lighting, lavishly decorated, and projecting an appearance of strength and permanence. The structure of the building was entirely visible and fully integrated with its form. The structural system featured an immense concrete groin-vaulted ceiling supported on heavy walls and interior columns. The ceiling incorporated coffers, which reduced weight while also contributing to the aesthetic effect. The groined vaulting allowed for large windows to be placed high on the walls of the main hall, facilitating natural lighting. The thrust of the vaults was restrained by perpendicular buttress vaults, which also contributed to the vastness of the interior by providing 6 additional rooms extending from the main hall. Thus all principal aspects of form, except the lavish interior décor, derived directly from the highly sophisticated structural system.

2. Roman engineers provided lateral support to arch bridges by building heavy stone foundations into the sides of river banks. They made extensive use of arcades, in which the lateral thrust of adjacent arches counterbalanced each other. When arches were raised up on columns, as in triumphal arches, the columns were made wide and heavy to enhance their stability. Vaulted ceilings were often laterally supported by perpendicular buttress vaults.

3. The configuration of these 2 buildings, as well as the earlier Baths of Trajan (A.D. 104–109), suggests that Roman engineers designed by extrapolation from previous experience—by adopting successful concepts from past structures and extending them to achieve slightly longer spans and slightly greater heights with each new iteration. The process was entirely empirical (not science-based), and it was fundamentally cautious in nature, yet it resulted many extraordinary structures.

4. Any structure with an arch or vault can be thought of as incorporating Roman structural concepts. My personal favorite is the Gladesville Bridge in Sydney, Australia. When this bridge was built in 1964, its 1000-ft arch was the longest in the world. Yet this modern structure was constructed just as the Romans would have done it. A temporary centering was erected across the Parramatta River, and the main arch ring was built up from individual wedge-shaped voussoirs made of precast concrete. Each voussoir measured roughly 20 × 15 × 10 ft.

Lecture 12

1. The functions of a Gothic cathedral are to glorify God and to provide a large enclosed public space for worship. The form of a typical Gothic cathedral is characterized by great height, emphasized by vertical lines and slender columns; large window openings filled with stained glass; pointed arches integrated with ribbed groined vaults; flying buttresses surmounted by pinnacles; and rich sculptural decoration and detailing. The structure is, in effect, a 3-dimensional frame—a stone skeleton consisting of the arches and ribs of the ceiling, supported vertically by slender columns and supported laterally by flying buttresses, with pinnacles adding weight to the buttresses to improve their stability. Thus, most of the characteristic features of Gothic architecture derive directly from structural load-carrying demands. Form follows structure.

2. A buttress is both a column and a beam. The drawing below shows
    an arched vault supported on 2 buttresses. If we isolate 1 buttress (as
    shown at right), we can see that it is subjected to the weight of the
    vault, oriented downward, and the lateral thrust of the vault, oriented
    horizontally. The vertical force causes compression in the buttress. In
    this sense, it is a column. The horizontal force causes bending in the
    buttress. In this sense, it is a beam.

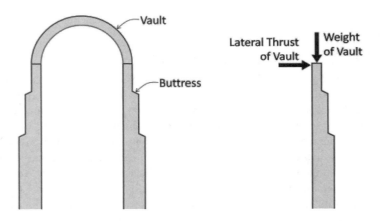

3. Flying buttresses are probably the most effective of the 4 Gothic-era
    innovations. Pointed arches and ribbed vaulting only serve to reduce
    the lateral thrust caused by the arches and vaults. They do nothing to
    resist that thrust. Flying buttresses resist thrust directly by providing a
    structural load path from the arches down to the foundations. Pinnacles
    only serve to improve the effectiveness of the buttresses by adding mass.

Lecture 13

1. The function of Brunelleschi's dome is to cover the crossing of the nave
    and transept of the cathedral. Its form is characterized by an octagonal
    plan and a tall profile—geometrically similar to a pointed Gothic arch.
    The dome is positioned on top of an octagonal drum and is surmounted
    by a heavy stone lantern. The structure of the dome consists of two shells
    with a space in between—an arrangement that reduces lateral thrust by

reducing the weight of the dome. The two shells are interconnected by 24 meridional ribs (only 8 of which are visible from the exterior) and 9 parallel (or horizontal) ribs. Embedded within the dome are 4 great chains—3 made of stone and 1 of timber—which are intended to resist lateral thrust and hoop stress. The only externally visible evidence of these chains is a series of square projections at the base of the dome. These are the ends of the cross-ties in the lower stone chain. The relationship between form and structure in this dome is complex. The tall profile of the dome is primarily a structural feature, which reduces lateral thrust and is significantly better suited to carrying the weight of the lantern than a hemispherical dome would have been. But all other aspects of the dome's form were dictated primarily by aesthetic, rather than structural, considerations. Indeed, these features—the octagonal plan, the position of the dome atop a tall drum, and the heavy stone lantern—are all structurally problematic. Most of Brunelleschi's engineering innovations were aimed at compensating for the adverse structural implications of these architectural features. And, except for the tall profile, these innovations are invisible—concealed within the masonry of the dome. Thus, for the most part, structure follows form in Brunelleschi's dome.

2. The spherical dome of the Pantheon generates considerable lateral thrust, which is resisted by thick layers of concrete around its base on the exterior of the structure. These layers of concrete obscure the shape of the dome from the outside. Thus the exterior of the dome does not look like a dome at all. Brunelleschi's dome resists lateral thrust through its taller profile, double-shell construction, ribs, and circumferential chains. None of these features mar or obscure the exterior appearance of the dome; thus, it can be appreciated at least as well from the outside of the building as from the inside.

3. Ribs and buttresses are also used to facilitate larger window openings in Gothic cathedrals.

4. The Treasury of Atreus is a corbelled dome. Just as a corbelled arch is known as a false arch, a corbelled dome is sometimes called a false dome. A corbelled dome is constructed by stacking successively smaller

rings of stone blocks on top of each other in horizontal layers. Individual stones carry load in flexure (because each stone is cantilevered inward from the layer of stones immediately below it), as well as compression (caused by the weight of the layers of stone above). The covered in this lecture are true domes, in that they carry load primarily through compression in the meridional direction. In the brick domes of Hagia Sophia and Santa Maria del Fiore, the layers of masonry are angled inward, perpendicular to the meridians, to facilitate the transmission of compressive force. The dome of the Pantheon is made of solid concrete and carries load as a true dome as well.

Lecture 14

1. The function of the Eads Bridge is to carry train and automobile traffic across the Mississippi River. Its form and structure are essentially indistinguishable. The overall configuration of the bridge and all of its individual elements directly reflect their load-carrying purposes. The main arch rings are constructed of hollow tubes, which are well suited to carry large compressive forces. Pairs of tubes are connected as trusses to improve their rigidity. The spandrels consist of vertical struts, which carry load directly from the deck to the main arches below. The abutments and piers are massive stone structures appropriately configured to carry the huge lateral thrust generated by the relatively flat arches. The Eads Bridge has no aesthetic adornments. It is, in a sense, pure structure.

2. Wooden structural components are cut from logs, and stone components are carved from stone blocks. In both cases, any material that is trimmed away is wasted. Thus, there is little cost saving to be gained from optimizing the size and shape of a wooden or stone structural element. In contrast, cast iron structural components are manufactured by pouring molten iron into a mold. Little or no material is wasted in the process. And even if an iron component needs to be cut to size or trimmed, any wasted material can be reheated and reused. Thus, the advent of mass-produced iron provided a powerful incentive to optimize structural elements by minimizing their weight. Our modern design philosophy emerged from this development. Science-based

design methods contributed to this design philosophy by providing the analytical tools necessary to predict optimum structural member sizes and configurations.

3. The overall shape of the Garabit Viaduct arches is parabolic—the optimum profile for a uniformly loaded arch. The crescent shape is formed by 2 parabolas that connect at the ends of the span and are spaced a maximum distance apart at mid-span. This configuration is well suited for carrying the large concentrated loads caused by locomotives crossing the span. Unlike uniform loads, concentrated loads cause an arch to bend. The tendency to bend (reflected in the internal moment) is greatest at mid-span and significantly less near the supports. Thus Eiffel's crescent shape provides maximum resistance to bending in the region of the arch where the internal moment is greatest.

Lecture 15

1. The function of the George Washington Bridge is to carry automobile traffic across the Hudson River. Like the Eads Bridge, the George Washington Bridge can be considered a pure structure: its form derives entirely from its structure. It is worth noting, however, that the original design of the bridge called for the 2 steel towers to be covered with a stone facade. Because funds ran short during the Great Depression, the facade was never added. Had it been built, we would see a divergence between form and structure in the George Washington Bridge. Its towers would appear to be solid stone but would, in fact, be supported by steel frameworks concealed behind the facade. Form usually follows structure in bridges; however, bridges designed to meet aesthetic goals sometimes include architectural features that are unrelated to structure. For example, the towers of the Golden Gate Bridge are adorned with Art Deco panels (highlighted below) that conceal trusses.

Photo Courtesy of Dr. Stephen Ressler.

2. Metal wire is manufactured by drawing it through successively smaller holes in a hardened metal plate. This process generally causes the wire to be stronger than the material from which it is manufactured. Thus a wire cable has greater strength per weight than an eyebar chain. A wire cable is also superior to an eyebar chain because of its greater redundancy. When a cable is built up from thousands of wires, the loss of a few wires due to corrosion or manufacturing defects will not significantly reduce the strength of the cable. In an eyebar chain, the loss of a single eyebar might easily cause the entire chain to fail.

3. The 2 most important structural characteristics of a modern suspension bridge cable are its internal configuration—thousands of parallel wires bundled together—and its attachment to the cable anchorages at the ends of the bridge. Neither of these characteristics is visible except from the interior of the anchorage structure, where few of us will ever have an opportunity to visit. Learning about the process used to fabricate the cables allows us to understand and appreciate these structural characteristics more fully, even if we are not able to see them.

Lecture 16

1. The Severn Bridge was originally designed with a conventional stiffening truss. Because of concerns about wind-induced vibration, a physical model of the truss was constructed for wind-tunnel testing. But during testing the model broke free from its mountings and was destroyed. While waiting for a replacement model to be built, the engineers did some experiments with very simple aerodynamically shaped box girders. The tests were unexpectedly successful, and so the design of the Severn Bridge was modified to incorporate an aerodynamic box girder, rather than a stiffening truss. The lessons we might learn from this event are, first, that innovation is not always planned and, second, that decision makers need to be willing to take advantage of such serendipitous discoveries when they occur.

Lecture 17

1. In engineering practice, human fallibility is accounted for, first and foremost, by ensuring that all engineering calculations are independently checked by another engineer. Failure to provide for adequate independent review was a major cause of the Quebec Bridge disaster.

Lecture 18

1. The function of the iron-framed British mill buildings was to enclose and facilitate industrial processes, while providing a higher level of fire resistance than had previous wood-framed mill buildings. Because these were utilitarian buildings, their design was not significantly influenced by aesthetic considerations. Thus, their form was largely dictated by function (e.g., the use of many large windows to provide natural lighting) and structure (e.g., subdivision of the building into many identical rectangular bays, so that standardized iron structural components could be used). Even though structural considerations dominated the design of these buildings, some of the most interesting aspects of their structural systems are typically not visible because their brick jack arch floor systems completely enclose the supporting beams.

2. The early British mill buildings are great structures because they represent landmarks in engineering innovation. They deserve our attention, in part, because they were instrumental in the development of the modern skyscraper, but also because they are historically important in their own right.

3. When iron-framed buildings developed in the late 18th and early 19th centuries, iron represented a clear improvement over the timber framing that had previously been used for the interior structure of buildings. But in these buildings, there was no compelling reason to stop using traditional masonry exterior walls. Iron did not offer better fire resistance than masonry, and even if exterior iron framing had been used, the open spaces between the beams and columns would have required masonry walls anyway. This situation did not change significantly until the advent of taller buildings in the 1870s. As a building gets taller, load-bearing exterior walls must necessarily get thicker to ensure their stability. When a building's height approaches 10 stories, masonry load-bearing walls become so thick that they impinge significantly on floor space. In the 1870s, builders' desire to maximize interior floor space for a given building footprint provided the economic incentive for replacing masonry exterior walls with iron and steel framing.

Lecture 19

1. The principal function of both the Empire State Building and the John Hancock Center is to provide a large amount of commercial office space for a relatively small building footprint. The form of the Empire State Building (and other skyscrapers of its era) was designed to achieve an aesthetic effect, largely independent of structure. Structure follows form in this building. The form of the John Hancock Center (and other skyscrapers of the Second Chicago School) is largely dependent on the structure. The columns, beams, and cross-bracing elements dominate the exterior appearance of the building and clearly communicate their load-carrying purpose. Form follows structure in this building.

2. Egyptian pyramids, Roman basilicas, Gothic cathedrals, and skyscrapers all reflect the innate human aspiration to build upward, and in each case the structure's height had the symbolic function of glorifying a person or institution. The pyramids glorified the pharaoh; grand basilicas glorified the emperor; cathedrals glorified God and the church; and the early 20th-century skyscrapers glorified corporations and their owners.

3. The Bank of China Tower, constructed between 1985 and 1990, was the tallest building in Asia and the fifth tallest in the world at the time it was built. Its design engineer has characterized the structural system as a bundled vertical space truss. It consists of 4 trussed tubes, triangular in plan, combined to form a square footprint at the base of the building. These 4 triangular tubes extend upward to different heights, creating a building profile that looks substantially different when viewed from the four points of the compass. Thus the Bank of China Tower represents a unique blend of the structural systems used in the John Hancock Center (a single trussed tube) and the Sears Tower (9 framed tubes bundled

together). Another unique aspect of the Bank of China Tower is that all principal elements of the bundled vertical space truss system are steel members encased in concrete. The principal purpose of the concrete is to improve the fire resistance of the system.

Lecture 20

1. The innovative structure of the Ingalls Building—the world's first reinforced concrete skyscraper—is largely concealed behind a traditional facade of marble on the first 3 stories, glazed brick on the next 11, and terra-cotta on the top story and cornice. Thus, structure follows form in this building.

2. For the 2-span continuous beam below, steel reinforcing bars would be required at the locations indicated with dashed lines. Under uniform loading, this beam will bend concave downward in the vicinity of the center support and concave upward everywhere else. Where the flexure is concave downward, tension occurs on the top of the beam; thus, the reinforcement must be placed on top. Where the flexure is concave upward, tension occurs on the bottom of the beam; thus, the reinforcement must be placed on the bottom.

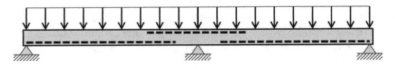

The two layers of reinforcement overlap because reinforcing bars must always be extended beyond the regions in which they are required for tension reinforcement. This practice ensures that the ends of the bars are soundly anchored in compressed concrete.

3. The tension in a post-tensioning cable causes compression in the surrounding concrete. Thus, post tensioning can eliminate or sharply reduce cracking in concrete beams by offsetting the tensile stresses that normally occur in flexure. Post tensioning can also significantly reduce bending deformations—an important benefit because concrete is

significantly less stiff than steel. Finally, when used in conjunction with precast segmental construction, post tensioning allows long-span beams to be built without the use of temporary supports or formwork.

4. The bridge is a post-tensioned segmental box-girder structure. Concrete is well suited to the complex geometry of the girders, which are curved in profile, curved in plan (i.e., when viewed from above), and trapezoidal in cross-section. The use of post-tensioned segmental construction allowed the structure to be built without any temporary supports—a particularly important consideration for such a tall bridge. In addition, the vertical piers have a unique sculpted quality that could only have been achieved in concrete.

Lecture 21

1. In the 3-part dome of St. Paul's Cathedral, the structure—a brick cone— is entirely concealed between nonstructural interior and exterior domes. Christopher Wren added these outer and inner shells only to improve the appearance of the dome. Thus, structure follows form in the dome of St. Paul's. In Chapel Lomas de Cuernavaca, the form and structure are inseparable. The structure is a thin concrete hypar shell. Its graceful form derives entirely from the hypar shape, which is a fundamentally structural configuration. Thus, form follows structure in this building.

2. In comparison with traditional masonry vaulting, the timbrel vault is much lighter; thus, its lateral thrust is significantly smaller. And unlike traditional masonry, the timbrel vault can be constructed without any temporary centering.

3. Because of their extraordinary structural efficiency, thin-shell structures have low material cost. However, because of their complex shapes, thin shells also tend to have high construction costs. In particular, the labor costs associated with constructing complex formwork are likely to be significant. This is one reason why thin-shall structures have been used more extensively in Mexico than in the U.S. In Mexico, labor costs tend to be relatively lower in comparison with material costs.

4. The work of Eduardo Torroja, Felix Candela, and Pier Nervi suggests that thin shells are most effective when their shape is defined to accomplish a specific structural purpose. In other words, thin shells work best when form follows structure. The roof of the Sydney Opera House was designed, first and foremost, to achieve a certain aesthetic effect: The curved shells were intended to resemble the sails of a boat. As a result, they were oriented vertically, and each was supported principally on 2 corners. Because of this unusual configuration, thin-shell construction proved to be structurally infeasible. The roof elements were ultimately designed and built as frames, which were better suited to the demands of Jørn Utzon's architectural concept. In the Sydney Opera House, structure followed form, and the utility of thin-shell construction was compromised as a result.

Lecture 22

1. The dome of the Paris Grain Market is a grid of meridional and parallel ribs. Under load, the meridional ribs work like arches, carrying load in compression, while the lower parallel ribs carry hoop stress in tension. Thus, the meridional ribs are made of cast iron, which is strong in compression, and the parallel ribs are wrought iron, which is stronger in tension. The perpendicular elements of the dome's simple grid configuration reflect the distinctly different properties of the 2 available materials. The Houston Astrodome is made of steel, which exhibits no significant difference between its strengths in tension and compression. Thus, a more complex geometric configuration could be used with no difficulty. In addition, the greater strength of steel allowed for a significantly longer span and a significantly flatter profile, with the large lateral thrust being restrained by a circumferential steel tension ring.

2. Science-based design is reflected in the shapes of the trusses that reinforce the basket-handle arches of the east-west train hall. These trusses perfectly match the moment diagram of the arch under uniform loading. Thus they provide appropriate flexural strength with extraordinary structural efficiency.

Lecture 23

1. Both roofs are saddle-shaped, and thus they both share the dramatic appearance of the hypar form. From a structural perspective, however, they are exact opposites. Chapel Lomas de Cuernavaca is a concrete thin-shell structure, which carries load primarily in compression. Its supports must restrain the outward thrust of parabolic shell. The Dorton Arena roof is a tension structure, composed of steel cables configured as a perpendicular grid and covered with metal cladding. Its supports (the 2 massive concrete arches) must restrain the inward pull of the cables.

2. The shape of the cables constituting the hanging dish roof system is identical to the optimum profile of a dome—a catenary. In every other respect, the hanging dish and the dome are structural opposites. The orientation of the dish is concave upward; the dome is concave downward. The dish is laterally restrained by a compression ring, the dome by a tension ring (e.g., the chains embedded within Brunelleschi's dome in Florence). The central element in the hanging dish is a tension ring, while a dome uses a compression ring (e.g., the oculus of the Pantheon).

3. The structural components of a bicycle wheel are the hub (which includes the axle), the rim, and the spokes. After the spokes are installed, they are post tensioned. When the spokes are tensioned, the wheel is kept in equilibrium through compression in the rim and tension in the hub.

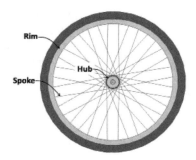

When the wheel is mounted on a bicycle, the weight of the bike and its rider causes a downward force on the axle, which is counterbalanced by an upward reaction at the point of contact between the tire and the road (as shown below). The effect of these 2 forces is to compress the vertical spokes immediately below the hub. Had these spokes not been post tensioned, they would experience axial compression, and because they are so slender, they would buckle. However, because of the post tensioning, the external loading only causes a reduction of the tension in these spokes. The internal tension due to post tensioning is greater than the compressive effect of the external loads. Thus the combined effect is a net tension force, and the spokes do not buckle.

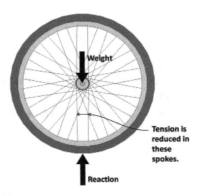

The Utica Auditorium is quite similar to a bicycle wheel, in that it is composed of an inner tension ring (the hub), an outer compression ring (the rim), and tensioned cables (the spokes). Its primary difference is in the direction of loading. A bicycle wheel is loaded in the plane of the wheel, while the Utica Auditorium roof is loaded in perpendicular to the plane of the wheel. Also, the Utica Auditorium roof uses vertical struts to maintain the tension in the cable, while bicycle spokes are tensioned by threaded connectors at their ends. Nonetheless, despite these differences, the component parts of both systems carry load in essentially the same way.

4. The Kurilpa Bridge is a true tensegrity structure. It is composed of compression struts interconnected with pretensioned cables. No 2 compression struts are connected directly to each other, and to maintain

the stability and rigidity of the structure, at least 3 tension cables are connected to each end of each compression strut. In this sense, the Kurilpa Bridge carries load in exactly the same way as David Geiger's cable dome at the Seoul Gymnastics Hall. The only significant difference between the 2 structures is that Geiger's dome uses a regular geometric configuration, while the Kurilpa Bridge is deliberately irregular.

Lecture 24

1. The function of the Hoover Dam is to hold back an immense wall of water, which is used to generate hydroelectric power. The structure of the dam is an immense concrete arch, turned sideways such that it carries load in compression to the walls of the canyon. The canyon walls serve as foundations, carrying both the net lateral pressure of the water (a force oriented in the downstream direction) and the outward thrust of the dam. The form of the dam derives entirely from its structure.

2. Cable-stayed bridges are superficially similar to suspension bridges in that both are tension structures that use cables and towers as principal load-carrying elements. However, as structural systems, the 2 bridge types are substantially different. The principal differences are summarized in the table below.

Cable-Stayed Bridge	Suspension Bridge
Cables are straight.	Cables are draped.
Cables are attached directly to stiffening girder.	Stiffening girder or truss is supported by vertical suspenders, which are attached to the main cables.
Cables cause compression in stiffening girder.	Cables cause no compression in stiffening girder or truss.
Cables are anchored to the bridge.	Cables require external anchorages.
Cables are directly attached to towers; thus, they apply significant lateral loads to the towers.	Cables pass over the tops of towers; thus, they apply significantly less lateral load.
Structure is relatively stiff.	Structure is relatively flexible.
Typically used for medium spans (500–2000 ft).	Typically used for long spans (more than 2000 ft).

Great Structures Discussed in this Course

Year Completed	Structure	Design Engineer	Location	Importance
27th century B.C.	Meidum Pyramid		Meidum, Egypt	Early step pyramid convert-ed to a true pyramid, but it subsequently collapsed.
26th century B.C.	Great Pyramid		Giza, Egypt	World's tallest structure from the time of its construction un-til the 14th century A.D.; only one of the Seven Wonders of the Ancient World that has survived to modern times.
21st century B.C.	Ziggurat of Ur		Iraq	Monumental ancient mud brick structure.
c. 1250 B.C.	Treasury of Atreus		Mycenae, Greece	Excellent example of an ancient corbelled dome.
c. 1250 B.C.	Lion Gate		Mycenae, Greece	Excellent example of an ancient corbelled arch
550 B.C.	Temple of Hera		Paestum, Italy	Early Greek temple in the Doric style; interior columns are placed in the center of the cella.
5th century B.C.	Temple of Artemis		Ephesus, Turkey	Monumental Greek temple; one of the Seven Wonders of the Ancient World.
432 B.C.	Parthenon	Phidias	Athens, Greece	Most famous of all Greek tem-ples; built in the Doric style.

Year Completed	Structure	Design Engineer	Location	Importance
406 B.C.	Erechtheion		Athens, Greece	Greek temple in the Ionic style.
62 B.C.	Pons Fabricius		Rome, Italy	Oldest fully intact Roman bridge.
1st century B.C.	Pont-Saint-Martin		Pont-Saint-Martin, Italy	Probably the longest-spanning arch that has survived from antiquity.
1st century B.C.	Pont du Gard		Nîmes, France	Monumental Roman aqueduct.
c. 80	Colosseum		Rome, Italy	Monumental arena employing multiple barrel vaults; velarium (awning) was an early example of a tension structure.
81	Arch of Titus		Rome, Italy	Excellent example of a Roman triumphal arch.
c. 100	Segovia Aqueduct		Segovia, Spain	Monumental Roman aqueduct.
113	Trajan's Column		Rome, Italy	Monumental Roman stone column commemorating Trajan's victory over the Dacians.

Great Structures Discussed in this Course

Year Completed	Structure	Design Engineer	Location	Importance
126	Pantheon	Apollodorus of Damascus	Rome, Italy	World's largest dome from time of its construction until the 19th century; demonstrates adept use of concrete as a structural material.
3rd century	Baths of Caracalla		Rome, Italy	Excellent example of monumental Roman vaulted basilica.
324	St. Paul's Basilica		Rome, Italy	Early Christian basilica; demonstrates the use of timber roof trusses in Roman structures.
310	Basilica of Maxentius		Rome, Italy	Excellent example of monumental Roman vaulted basilica; 3 buttress vaults remain.
c. 310	Basilica of Constantine		Trier, Germany	Largest intact basilica surviving from antiquity.
532	Hagia Sophia		Istanbul, Turkey	World's finest example of Byzantine architecture; world's largest cathedral for 1000 years after its construction.
c. 540	Persian Imperial Palace at Ctesiphon		Iraq	Extraordinary parabolic brick vault, constructed without centering.
8th–10th centuries	Great Mosque of Córdoba		Córdoba, Spain	Example of early use of pointed arches in Islamic architecture.
11th century	Rainbow Bridge		China	Traditional timber-framed structure, often mistakenly called an arch.

Year Completed	Structure	Design Engineer	Location	Importance
1004	San Giovenale		Orvieto, Italy	Excellent example of early Romanesque basilica; uses simple triangulated wooden roof trusses.
1013	San Miniato al Monte		Florence, Italy	Excellent example of early Romanesque basilica; incorporates several ancient Roman columns.
1031	Krak des Chevaliers		Syria	Greatest of the Crusader castles in the Levant; excellent example of medieval military architecture.
1031	St. Michael's Church		Hildesheim, Germany	Excellent example of early Romanesque basilica.
1061	Speyer Cathdral		Speyer, Germany	World's largest intact Romanesque structure; among the earliest Romanesque buildings to use groined vaulting.
12th–13th centuries	Cathedral of Our Lady at Chartres		Chartres, France	High Gothic cathedral that incorporates an earlier Romanesque facade; heavy flying buttresses allow for unusually large windows.
12th–15th centuries	Cathedral of St. Stephen at Bourges		Bourges, France	High Gothic cathedral; slender flying buttresses with unique double pinnacles.

Great Structures Discussed in this Course

Year Completed	Structure	Design Engineer	Location	Importance
1196	Trier Cathedral		Trier, Germany	West façade exhibits many typical Romanesque architectural features; portions of the building date from the 4th century.
13th century	Cathedral of Our Lady at Amiens		Amiens, France	Tallest complete Gothic nave in France (second only to Beauvais cathedral, which is incomplete).
13th century	Cathedral of Our Lady at Coutances		Coutances, France	High Gothic cathedral with a unique octagonal tower at the crossing of nave and transept.
13th–14th centuries	Cathedral of Our Lady at Reims		Reims, France	High Gothic cathedral, famous as the place where the kings of France were crowned; slender flying buttresses with particularly heavy pinnacles.
13th–15th centuries	Cathedral of Our Lady at Strasbourg		Strasbourg, France	High Gothic cathedral that incorporates earlier Romanesque choir and transept; world's tallest building from 1647 to 1874.
13th–16th centuries	Cathedral of St. Peter and St. Paul at Troyes		Troyes, France	Typical example of a High Gothic cathedral.

Year Completed	Structure	Design Engineer	Location	Importance
13th–16th centuries	Cathedral of St. Pierre at Beauvais		Beauvais, France	World's tallest vaulted nave; collapsed in 1284 and was repaired but never completed.
1359	Campanile of Santa Maria del Fiore	Giotto	Florence, Italy	Medieval bell tower; masterpiece of Florentine Gothic architecture.
1436	Dome of Santa Maria del Fiore	Filippo Brunelleschi	Florence, Italy	World's largest brick dome; highly innovative 2-shell ribbed design.
c. 1460	Pazzi Chapel	Filippo Brunelleschi	Florence, Italy	Regarded as one of the most perfectly proportioned buildings of the Italian Renaissance; model of exemplary form.
1514	Campanile of San Marco		Venice, Italy	Hollow masonry tower; model for numerous modern structures, including the MetLife Tower (1909).
1711	St. Paul's Cathedral	Christopher Wren, Robert Hooke	London, U.K.	Highly efficient dome design, with 1 structural and 2 nonstructural shells.
1752	Cistercian Monastery of Santa Maria de Alcobaça		Alcobaça, Portugal	First known use of cast iron columns.
1779	Iron Bridge	Abraham Darby III	Coalbrookdale, U.K.	World's first iron bridge.

Great Structures Discussed in this Course

Year Completed	Structure	Design Engineer	Location	Importance
1790	Théâtre Français		Paris, France	World's first wrought iron roof trusses.
1793	Strutt's Mill	William Strutt	Belper, U.K.	Innovative structural system, using iron columns, iron-sheathed wooden beams, and brick arched floor system with iron tie rods.
1797	Bage's Mill	Charles Bage	Shrewsbury, U.K.	Innovative structural system; improved on Strutt's mill by using iron beams.
1800	White House	James Hoban	Washington DC	A neoclassical building made famous by its function as home to the President of the United States.
1801	Jacob's Creek Bridge	James Finley	Uniontown, PA	World's first suspension bridge capable of carrying vehicular traffic.
1809	Newburyport Bridge	James Finley	Newburyport, MA	Only surviving suspension bridge designed by James Finley (mostly reconstructed).
1813	Paris Grain Market		Paris, France	World's first long-span iron roof—an iron ribbed dome.
1817	Union Bridge	Samuel Brown	New Waterford, U.K.	World's first eyebar chain suspension bridge.

Year Completed	Structure	Design Engineer	Location	Importance
1823	Saint-Antoine Bridge	Guillaume Henri Dufour	Geneva, Switzerland	World's first permanent wire cable suspension bridge.
1823	Chain Pier	Samuel Brown	Brighton, U.K.	Pier constructed as a suspension bridge; destroyed by wind in 1896.
1826	Menai Strait Bridge	Thomas Telford	Anglesey, U.K.	Among the finest early iron-chain suspension bridges.
1834	Orrell's Mill	Eaton Hodgkinson	Stockport, U.K.	Innovative structural system; world's first scientifically designed cast-iron beams.
1834	Grand Pont Suspendu	Joseph Chaley	Fribourg, Switzerland	Early wire-cable suspension bridge; world's longest span at the time of its construction.
1837	Euston Station		London	Probably the world's first triangulated wrought iron truss.
1839	Basse-Chaîne Bridge	Joseph Chaley	Angers, France	Early wire-cable suspension bridge; collapsed in 1850, setting back French suspension bridge development by 20 years.
1841	Whipple Bowstring Truss	Squire Whipple	Schenectady, NY	First scientifically designed truss in the United States.
1847	Delaware River Aqueduct	John Roebling	Lackawaxen, PA	Oldest wire cable suspension bridge in the United States.

Great Structures Discussed in this Course

Year Completed	Structure	Design Engineer	Location	Importance
1849	Wheeling Bridge	Charles Ellet	Wheeling, WV	World's longest bridge at the time of its construction; collapsed in 1854 due to wind-induced vibration.
1850	Britannia Bridge		Wales	Innovative continuous iron box-girder structure.
1855	Niagara Gorge Bridge	John Roebling	Niagara Falls, NY	First suspension bridge to successfully carry a railroad.
1857	E.V. Haughwout Building	Daniel Badger	New York, NY	Excellent example of cast-iron facade.
1859	Iron Storage Building, Watervliet Arsenal		Watervliet, NY	Oldest all-iron building in the United States.
1859	Royal Albert Bridge	I. K. Brunel	Saltash, U.K.	Innovative lenticular truss design; model for the modern University of Phoenix Stadium roof.
1866	U.S. Capitol Dome	T. U. Walter	Washington DC	Three-part dome adapted from St. Paul's Cathedral, London.
1868	St. Pancras Station		London, U.K.	World's longest single-span roof at the time of its construction.

Year Completed	Structure	Design Engineer	Location	Importance
1870	Equitable Life Assurance Building	George Post	New York, NY	Important milestone in early skyscraper development; early use of interior iron framing in a commercial (rather than industrial) building.
1874	Eads Bridge	James Eads	St. Louis, MO	World's first bridge to use steel structural components; world's longest arch at the time of its construction.
1878	Firth of Tay Bridge	Thomas Bouch	Firth of Tay, U.K.	World's longest bridge at the time of its construction; collapsed in 1879.
1879	First Leiter Building	W. L. Jenney	Chicago, IL	Important milestone in early skyscraper development; first use of exterior iron columns in a tall building.
1883	Brooklyn Bridge	John Augustus Roebling, Washington Roebling	New York, NY	World's longest span at the time of its construction; model for all modern suspension bridges.
1884	Garabit Viaduct	Gustave Eiffel	Massif Central, France	World's longest arch at the time of its construction; design strongly reflects structural load-carrying principles.

Great Structures Discussed in this Course

Year Completed	Structure	Design Engineer	Location	Importance
1885	Home Insurance Building	W. L. Jenney	Chicago, IL	Important milestone in early skyscraper development; first fully integrated iron structural frame in a tall building.
1886	Statue of Liberty	Gustave Eiffel	New York, NY	Complex internal iron-framed structural system.
1887	Chouteau Bridge		Kansas City, MO	Excellent example of Whipple trapezoidal truss configuration.
1889	Eiffel Tower	Gustave Eiffel	Paris, France	World's tallest tower at the time of its construction; icon of the city of Paris.
1890	Firth of Forth Bridge	John Fowler, Benjamin Baker	Firth of Forth, U.K.	World's first all-steel bridge; pioneering cantilever design; both spans were the world's longest at the time of their construction.
1891	Wainwright Building	Louis Sullivan	Chicago, IL	Excellent example of Chicago School architecture.
1901	Zuoz Bridge	Robert Maillart	Zuoz, Switzerland	World's first concrete box-girder bridge.
1903	Ingalls Building	H. N. Hooper	Cincinnati, OH	World's first reinforced concrete skyscraper.

Year Completed	Structure	Design Engineer	Location	Importance
1904	Saint Jean de Mont-martre		Paris, France	Excellent example of early rein-forced concrete structure; unique Art Nouveau architectural detailing implemented in concrete.
1907	First Quebec Bridge	Theodore Cooper	Quebec Province, Canada	Collapsed during construction; would have been the world's longest span.
1907	Great Mosque at Djenne		Djenne, Mali	World's largest mud-brick struc-ture.
1908	Singer Building		New York, NY	World's tallest building at the time of its construction; designed in the Beaux-Arts style.
1909	MetLife Tower		New York, NY	World's tallest building at the time of its construction; designed to re-semble the medieval campanile of San Marco in Venice.
1909	Queensboro Bridge	Gustav Lindenthal	New York, NY	Excellent example of an early canti-lever truss bridge.
1913	Woolworth Building		New York, NY	World's tallest building at the time of its construction; designed in the Neo-Gothic style.

Great Structures Discussed in this Course

Year Completed	Structure	Design Engineer	Location	Importance
1917	Second Quebec Bridge		Quebec Province, Canada	World's longest cantilever bridge; redesigned version of the bridge that collapsed in 1907.
1922	Zeiss Planetarium	Walter Bauersfeld	Jena, Germany	World's first geodesic dome; first scientifically designed thin-shell structure.
1924	Bear Mountain Bridge		Stony Point, NY	World's longest-spanning suspension bridge at the time of its construction.
1930	Salginatobel Bridge	Robert Maillart	Schiers, Switzerland	Masterpiece of reinforced concrete bridge design.
1930	Bank of Manhattan Trust Building		New York, NY	World's tallest building at the time of its construction.
1930	Chrysler Building		New York, NY	World's tallest building at the time of its construction.
1931	Empire State Building		New York, NY	World's tallest building at the time of its construction; currently the tallest building in New York City.
1931	George Washington Bridge	Othmar Ammann	New York, NY	World's longest bridge at the time of its construction.
1932	Nebraska State Capitol	Bertram Goodhue	Lincoln, NE	Excellent example of 20th-century stone masonry bearing-wall structure.

Year Completed	Structure	Design Engineer	Location	Importance
1935	Madrid Hippodrome	Eduardo Torroja	Madrid, Spain	Early thin-shell concrete structure; innovative hypar/cantilever roof.
1935	Hoover Dam		Arizona-Nevada border, U.S.	Monumental concrete structure; one of the 20th century's greatest construction achievements.
1936	Hersheypark Arena	Anton Tedesko	Hershey, PA	World's longest-spanning cylindrical shell roof at the time of its construction.
1937	Golden Gate Bridge	Joseph B. Strauss, Charles A. Ellis	San Francisco, CA	World's longest bridge at the time of its construction.
1937	Fallingwater	Frank Lloyd Wright	Mill Run, PA	One of America's greatest architectural works; concrete cantilever balconies were structurally inadequate as designed.
1940	Tacoma Narrows Bridge	Leon Moisseiff	Puget Sound, WA	Famously destroyed by wind-induced vibration in July 1940.
1952	J. S. Dorton Arena	Matthew Nowicki, Fred Severud	Raleigh, NC	World's first cable-supported roof.
1953	Schwarzwaldhalle	Ulrich Finsterwalder	Karlsruhe, Germany	Innovative saddle-shaped thin-shell concrete roof.
1953	Kresge Auditorium	Eero Saarinen	Cambridge, MA	Innovative dome-shaped thin-shell concrete roof.

Great Structures Discussed in this Course

Year Completed	Structure	Design Engineer	Location	Importance
1956	Strömsund Bridge	Franz Dischinger	Strömsund, Sweden	World's first modern cable-stayed bridge.
1957	Palazzetto dello Sport	Pier Luigi Nervi	Rome, Italy	Innovative ribbed thin-shell roof, constructed of *ferrocemento*; innovative structural system with V-shaped flying buttresses.
1958	David S. Ingalls Hockey Rink	Eero Saarinen	New Haven, CT	Innovative cable-supported roof.
1958	Chapel Lomas de Cuernavaca	Felix Candela	Cuernavaca, Mexico	Innovative thin-shell concrete hyperbolic... ar structure.
1959	Utica Memorial Auditorium		Utica, NY	Innovative bicycle wheel cable-supported roof.
1959	Solomon R. Guggenheim Museum	Frank Lloyd Wright	New York, NY	Important 20th-century architectural landmark; demonstrates concrete's versatility of form.
1960	Palazzo dello Sport	Pier Luigi Nervi	Rome, Italy	Innovative ribbed thin-shell roof, constructed of *ferrocemento*.
1962	Trans World Flight Center	Eero Saarinen	New York, NY	Innovative thin-shell concrete structure.
1965	Houston Astrodome		Houston, TX	World's first domed stadium.

Year Completed	Structure	Design Engineer	Location	Importance
1965	Gateway Arch	Eero Saarinen	Saint Louis, MO	Monumental catenary arch.
1966	Severn Bridge		South Gloucestershire, U.K.	World's first suspension bridge to use an aerodynamically designed stiffening girder.
1968	Madison Square Garden		New York, NY	Innovative hanging dish roof system.
1970	John Hancock Center	Fazlur Khan	Chicago, IL	Excellent example of Second Chicago School skyscraper; trussed tube structural system.
1971	Cathedral of Saint Mary of the Assumption		San Francisco, CA	Innovative roof system composed of four vertically oriented hypar concrete shells.
1972	Olympiapark	Frei Otto	Munich, Germany	Pioneering tension structures with cable-supported membrane roofs.
1972	World Trade Center		New York, NY	Excellent example of framed tube structural system; destroyed by terrorist attack in 2001.
1973	Sydney Opera House	Jorn Utzon	Sydney, Australia	Icon of the city of Sydney; characteristic curved roof elements are actually reinforced concrete frames, not thin shells.

Great Structures Discussed in this Course

Year Completed	Structure	Design Engineer	Location	Importance
1973	Minneapolis Federal Reserve Building (currently Marquette Plaza)		Minneapolis, MN	Innovative use of draped parabolic cable in a building structural system.
1974	Sears Tower	Fazlur Khan	Chicago, IL	Excellent example of Second Chicago School skyscraper; framed tube structural system; world's tallest building at the time of its construction.
1975	Hartford Civic Center		Hartford, CT	Large space truss roof system; collapsed in 1978 due to design errors.
1976	CN Tower		Toronto, Canada	World's tallest structure at the time of its construction.
1977	Citigroup Center	William LeMessurier	New York, NY	Highly unusual structural system; nearly collapsed due to design errors.
1980	Ganter Bridge	Christian Menn	Switzerland	Highly innovative segmental concrete cable-stayed bridge.

Year Completed	Structure	Design Engineer	Location	Importance
1983	Linn Cove Viaduct	Eugene Figg	Grandfather Mountain, NC	First post-tensioned concrete segmental bridge in the United States.
1987	Sunshine Skyway Bridge	Eugene Figg	Tampa Bay, FL	Innovative post-tensioned concrete segmental cable-stayed bridge.
1988	Olympic Gymnastics Hall	David H. Geiger	Seoul, South Korea	World's first cable-dome structural system.
1989	Louvre Pyramid	I. M. Pei	Paris, France	Glass-clad space truss.
1990	Broadgate Exchange House		London, U.K.	Innovative use of a parabolic steel arch in a building structural system.
1991	Olympic Velodrome	Santiago Calatrava	Athens, Greece	Arena featuring an innovative roof system suspended from 2 tubular arches.
1992	Alamillo Bridge	Santiago Calatrava	Seville, Spain	Innovative and aesthetically striking single-tower cable-stayed bridge.
1994	Chunnel		English Channel	Modern concrete-reinforced railroad tunnel.
1997	Campo Volantin	Santiago Calatrava	Bilbao, Spain	Innovative and aesthetically striking steel tied-arch bridge.

Great Structures Discussed in this Course

Year Completed	Structure	Design Engineer	Location	Importance
1997	Guggenheim Museum	Frank Gehry	Bilbao, Spain	Regarded as an architectural masterpiece; structure is entirely hidden within apparently random shapes and a titanium skin.
1998	Raftsundet Bridge		Lofoten, Norway	World's longest beam bridge at the time of its construction; elegant concrete box-girder design.
1998	Petronas Towers		Kuala Lumpur, Malaysia	First concrete building to be the world's tallest.
1998	Millennium Dome		London, U.K.	Innovative cable-stayed roof system.
1998	Akashi Kaikyō Bridge		Kobe, Japan	World's longest bridge.
2003	Auditorio de Tenerife	Santiago Calatrava	Tenerife, Canary Islands	Extraordinary thin-shell concrete roof.
2004	Millau Bridge		Millau, France	World's tallest bridge; multi-span cable-stayed structure.
2006	Berlin Hauptbahnhof		Berlin, Germany	Largest train station in Europe; innovative, structurally optimal long-span arch system.

Year Completed	Structure	Design Engineer	Location	Importance
2006	University of Phoenix Stadium		Phoenix, AZ	Massive lenticular roof trusses modeled on Brunel's Royal Albert Bridge of 1859.
2006	Turning Torso Tower	Santiago Calatrava	Malmo, Sweden	High-rise building modeled on a twisting human form; unique external truss.
2008	Beijing Capital International Airport		Beijing, China	Excellent example of modern optimally designed columns.
2009	Samuel Beckett Bridge	Santiago Calatrava	Dublin, Ireland	Innovative and aesthetically striking single-tower cable-stayed bridge.
2010	Burj Khalifa		Dubai, United Arab Emirates	World's tallest building; innovative reinforced concrete structural system.
2012 (estimated)	Tokyo Sky Tree		Tokyo, Japan	Will be the world's tallest tower when completed.
2026 (estimated)	La Sagrada Familia	Antoni Gaudi	Barcelona, Span	Cathedral demonstrating the design of arches using draped cables; under construction since 1882, but still unfinished.

Timeline—Important Discoveries and Developments in Structural Engineering

27th century B.C. .... Construction of the first Egyptian pyramids—the first human achievements that can reasonably be characterized as products of engineering.

6th century B.C. .... Cast iron is made in China.

3rd century B.C. .... Romans adopt concrete as a structural material.

c. 25 B.C. .... Vitruvius writes *De architectura*, the oldest surviving work on engineering and construction from the ancient world.

1570... Palladio publishes *Four Books on Architecture*, which includes drawings of well-detailed triangulated truss bridges.

1586... Simon Stevin publishes the first proof of the principle of equilibrium.

1638... Galileo publishes *Two New Sciences*, which includes experiments on the strength of beams in flexure and wires in tension.

1676... Robert Hooke publishes the principle that a catenary is the optimum shape for an arch.

1678.. Hooke publishes the principle that
the relationship between load and
deformation in a material is linear.

1687.. Isaac Newton publishes *Mathematical
Principles of Natural Philosophy*,
which includes his 3 laws of motion.

1709.. Abraham Darby produces
iron with coke.

1752.. First known use of cast iron in
structural components at a Cistercian
monastery in Alcobaça, Portugal.

1757.. Leonhard Euler develops
his mathematical model
for column buckling.

1779.. World's first iron bridge is built by
Abraham Darby at Coalbrookedale.

1794.. École Polytechnique is founded
in France to support science-
based engineering.

1801.. James Finley builds the world's
first suspension bridge capable
of carrying vehicular traffic.

1817.. Samuel Brown builds the world's first
eyebar chain suspension bridge.

1822.. Augustin Cauchy formally defines
the concepts of stress and strain.

1823 .... Claude-Louis Navier publishes his landmark report on suspension bridge design; Guillaume Henri Dufour builds the world's first permanent wire cable suspension bridge.

1824 .... Joseph Aspdin patents a process for manufacturing Portland cement.

1826 .... Claude-Louis Navier publishes on his comprehensive theory of elastic flexure in beams.

1834 .... William Fairbairn and Eaton Hodgkinson develop the world's first fully scientifically designed cast-iron beams at Orrell's Mill.

1847 .... Squire Whipple publishes the first science-based analysis of trusses in *A Work on Bridge-Building*; John Roebling patents his system for fabricating wire cables in place on a suspension bridge.

1850 .... Collapse of the Basse-Chaîne wire-cable suspension bridge at Angers, France, ends development of suspension bridges for the next 20 years in France.

1856 .... The Bessemer Process for making steel is developed.

1871 .... Great Chicago Fire stimulates a building boom in Chicago.

1874.. James Eads completes the
world's first major bridge to use
steel structural components.

1883.. Brooklyn Bridge is completed, firmly
establishing the construction methods
used in all modern suspension bridges.

1885.. William LeBaron Jenney builds the
world's first fully integrated iron
structural frame in a tall building;
Rafael Guastavino patents his tile
arch system, the timbrel vault.

1890.. John Fowler and Benjamin Baker
complete the Firth of Forth Bridge,
the world's first all-steel bridge.

1892.. Francois Hennebique patents his system
for reinforced concrete construction.

1903.. The Ingalls Building becomes
the world's first reinforced
concrete skyscraper.

1922.. Walter Bauersfeld completes the Zeiss
Dome—the world's first geodesic
dome and among the world's first
concrete thin-shell structures.

1940.. Tacoma Narrows Bridge collapses
due to wind-induced vibration,
stimulating the development of modern
wind-resistant suspension bridges.

1952.. Fred Severud completes the J. S. Dorton Arena, the world's first cable-supported roof.

1956.. Franz Dischinger completes the Strömsund Bridge, the world's first modern cable-stayed bridge.

1963.. Fazlur Khan designs the first framed-tube structural system (the DeWitt-Chestnut Apartments), which led to the skyscrapers of the Second Chicago School.

1965.. The Houston Astrodome becomes the world's first domed stadium.

1966.. The Severn Bridge becomes the world's first suspension bridge to use an aerodynamically designed stiffening girder.

1983.. Eugene Figg completes the Linn Cove Viaduct—the first post-tensioned concrete segmental bridge in the United States.

1988.. David H. Geiger completes the Gymnastics Hall for the Seoul Olympics, the world's first cable dome structural system.

1998.. The Petronas Towers in Malaysia become the first concrete buildings to be the world's tallest.

Glossary

aeroelastic flutter: A phenomenon in which an elastic body oscillates in response to air moving across it.

aggregate: Granular material (normally sand and gravel) used in concrete.

anchor arm: The portion of a cantilever bridge that counterbalances the cantilever arm.

anchorage: A structure that connects the main cables of a suspension bridge to the earth.

apse: The semicircular end of a basilica or church.

aqueduct: A structure that carries a water channel.

arcade: A row of adjacent arches, usually supported on columns.

arch: A structural element that, because of its shape and support configuration, carries load primarily in compression.

architrave: A horizontal stone beam spanning across the tops of the columns in a classical portico.

area moment of inertia: A measure of a cross-section's resistance to bending.

axial loading: A configuration in which a structural element is subjected only to loads aligned with its longitudinal axis. An axially loaded member must be either in tension or in compression.

barrel vault: A curved roof shaped like half of a cylinder, normally supported on two parallel walls.

bay: A rectangular module of a frame structure, formed by four columns.

beam: A structural element that is subjected to transverse loading and carries load in bending.

body: A physical object.

box girder: A beam with a hollow rectangular or trapezoidal cross-section.

braced frame: A frame that obtains its stability from diagonal bracing members or shear walls. A braced frame normally has pinned connections.

brittleness: Lack of ductility; the tendency of a material to fail suddenly and catastrophically, without plastic deformation.

buckling: A failure mode in which a member in compression suddenly deflects laterally and becomes unstable.

bundled tube system: A variation on the framed tube system that combines several framed tubes into a single structural system.

buttress: A thickened section of a wall that resists the lateral thrust of ceiling vaults.

buttress vault: A barrel vault used to restrain the lateral thrust of a larger vault, arch, or dome.

cable: A flexible structural element that carries load entirely in tension and changes its shape in response to the applied loading.

cable-stayed bridge: A bridge supported by straight cables radiating outward from one or more towers.

caldarium: The hot room in a Roman bath.

cantilever: (1) A beam supported at one end and unsupported at the other. The single support must prevent the supported end of the beam from rotating. (2) A construction technique in which halves of an arch or beam are

184

temporarily suspended from the ends of the span until they can be joined in the center.

cantilever arm: The portion of a cantilever bridge that projects beyond an intermediate support.

cantilever beam: A beam supported at one end and unsupported at the other. The single support must prevent the supported end of the beam from rotating.

capital: The decorative head on the top of a column.

cast iron: A construction material made by heating iron to the melting point and then pouring the liquid metal into a mold.

catenary: The curved shape of a draped cable subjected to a uniform loading distributed along the cable's length.

cella: The sanctuary of a Greek temple, housing a statue of the god or goddess to whom the temple is dedicated.

centering: A temporary structure used to support an arch while it is being constructed.

Chicago School: An architectural movement of the late 1800s and early 1900s that promoted the use of iron- and steel-frame structural systems in commercial buildings.

chord: A structural member that extends along the top or bottom of a truss.

clerestory: The uppermost level of a nave, containing a row of large windows.

coffer: A polygonal indentation in a vault, dome, or ceiling.

coke: A form of coal used as fuel in the manufacture of iron.

collonade: A grouping of columns placed at regular intervals.

column: A structural element that carries load primarily in compression; also called a compression member.

compression: An internal force that causes a structural element to shorten.

compression member: *See* **column**.

compression ring: A ring of masonry used to reinforce the oculus of a dome.

concrete: A material composed of a mixture of cement, water, and aggregate, which hardens into a strong, rock-like mass.

continuous beam: A beam supported at each end and extending continuously across one or more intermediate supports.

corbelled arch: A "false arch" constructed of horizontal layers of stone or brick. A corbelled arch is created by cantilevering successive layers of stone inward from each side of an opening, until they meet in the center.

corbelled dome: A dome built of horizontal layers of stone or brick. Each layer is a circular ring of masonry, and each successive layer is slightly smaller than the one below.

corrosion: Long-term deterioration of iron or steel caused by a chemical reaction with oxygen.

creep: The tendency of a material to experience long-term increases in deformation, even under a constant level of stress.

cross-section: The geometric shape formed by cutting through a structural element on a plane perpendicular to its length.

cross-sectional area: The area of a cross-section, expressed in units of length squared.

cruciform: Cross-shaped; this term is usually applied to the cross-section of a structural element.

dead load: A load that is permanent and unchanging. Dead load includes the weight of the structure itself, plus any nonstructural elements that are permanently attached to the structure.

deck truss: A truss bridge with the deck located at the level of the top chord.

deck: A flat structural element that directly supports a floor, roof, or roadway.

deformation: A change in the shape or dimensions of an object.

diagonal: A diagonally oriented truss member.

distributed load: A load that is spread uniformly along the length of the member. A distributed load is expressed in units of force per length.

drum: A cylindrical wall that supports a dome.

ductility: A material's capacity to undergo large, permanent deformations before failing, measured as the strain at fracture or the width of the material's stress-strain curve.

earthquake load: The effect of earthquake-induced ground motion on a structure.

effective length: The length of a compression member, measured between points of lateral support.

elastic: Material behavior characterized by non-permanent deformations. When a material is behaving elastically, load-induced deformations disappear when the load is removed.

empirical: Based on experience, observation, or experiment.

engineering: The application of math, science, and technology to create a system, component, or process that meets a human need.

entasis: A slight outward bulge in the middle of a classical column.

equilibrium: A condition in which all forces acting on a body are in balance. If a body is not moving (or is moving at a constant velocity), then it is in equilibrium.

eyebar chain: A chain composed of iron or steel bars linked together with pins.

factor of safety: A nondimensional measure of the safety of a structural element, calculated by dividing the failure stress (i.e., the strength) by the actual stress.

ferrocemento: A construction technique that used thin layers of concrete and wire mesh to create modular elements, which were then assembled by using cast-in-place concrete connections. *Ferrocemento* was developed by Pier Luigi Nervi.

flange: Horizontal element of an I-shaped cross-section.

flexure: The structural behavior of a beam, characterized by the deformation of the member into a curved shape, with compression occurring on the concave side and tension occurring on the convex side.

flying buttress: A structural element that resists the lateral thrust of ceiling vaults in a Gothic building. Flying buttresses are entirely external to the nave of the building they are supporting.

force: A push or a pull characterized by a magnitude and a direction. The magnitude of a force is measured in pounds in the U.S. system of units and in Newtons in the International System of units.

form: Appearance, reflected in physical features like shape, scale, proportion, and ornament.

frame: A structure composed of multiple members, at least one of which carries load in flexure.

framed-tube system: A type of structural system used in modern skyscrapers of the Second Chicago School. In the framed-tube system, a rigid external shell of beams and columns provides the lateral load-carrying capacity of the structure.

free-body diagram: A graphical problem-solving tool showing a body, isolated from its surroundings, annotated with all forces acting on that body.

frigidarium: The cold room in a Roman bath.

function: Purpose; how something is used by people.

groined vault: A vault formed by the intersection of two perpendicular barrel vaults.

hoop stress: Tension stress occurring in the parallel direction in a dome.

hyperbolic paraboloid (a.k.a. **hypar**): A saddle-like shape.

internal force: The force generated within a structural element in response to external forces. An internal force can be either tension or compression.

internal moment: A moment caused by the internal tension and compression forces in a beam.

jack arch: A flat arch.

lenticular truss: A lens-shaped truss.

live load: A load that varies in both magnitude and location. Live loads include occupancy, traffic, wind, snow, and earthquake loads.

load: An external force acting on a structure.

mechanics: The study of forces acting on bodies.

membrane: A synthetic fabric used as a structural element in a tension structure.

meridian: A line of longitude on a dome.

modulus of elasticity: A material property corresponding to the slope of the elastic portion of a stress-strain curve. It is a measure of the stiffness of a material.

moment diagram: A graph of internal moment versus length.

moment of a force: The tendency of a force to cause rotation about a point.

nave: The central hall of a church.

Newton's first law: A body at rest tends to remain at rest, unless it is acted on by an unbalanced force.

Newton's second law: An unbalanced force acting on a body causes the body to accelerate. The relationship between the force (F) and the acceleration (a) is given by the equation $F = ma$, where m is the mass of the body.

Newton's third law: For every action, there is an equal and opposite reaction.

occupancy load: The weight of people, furniture, and movable equipment in a building.

oculus: A circular opening at the top of a dome.

opus latericium: An ancient Roman building system in which concrete was placed between two brick outer walls.

parabola: The curved shape of a draped cable subjected to a uniform horizontally distributed loading.

parallel: A line of latitude on a dome.

pavimentum: A layer of granular material like crushed stone or tile, mixed with lime or cement, used as a road surface in Roman construction.

pendentive: A triangular element used to provide a smooth transition from a square bay to the circular base of a dome.

pinnacle: A pointed masonry element placed on top of a buttress.

pinned connection: A connection that allows the connected structural elements to rotate with respect to each other.

plate girder: An I-shaped beam constructed by riveting or welding individual plates or angles together.

plastic: Material behavior characterized by permanent deformations. When a material is behaving plastically, load-induced deformations remain, even after the load is removed.

polygon of forces: A graphical method of applying the principle of equilibrium. If a system of forces is in equilibrium, then those forces, drawn to scale, will form a closed polygon.

portico: A covered porch at the entrance of a building.

post tensioning: A system in which high-strength steel cables are threaded through holes or ducts in a precast concrete element, then tensioned with a hydraulic jack and anchored at their ends.

pozzolana: A volcanic ash used as cement in ancient Roman concrete.

profile: The shape of a structural element when viewed from the side.

reaction: An external force that occurs at a support to keep a structure or structural element in equilibrium.

reinforced concrete: Concrete strengthened with iron or steel bars in regions subjected to tensile stress.

relieving arch: An arch built into a wall above a door or window opening to divert compressive force around the opening.

rigid connection: A connection that restrains the connected structural elements from rotating with respect to each other.

rigid frame: A frame that obtains its stability from rigid connections between the beams and columns.

saddle: An iron or steel element that guides the main cables of a suspension bridge across the tops of the towers.

sand casting: A process for manufacturing metal objects by using a mold made of compacted sand.

Second Chicago School: An architectural movement that originated in the 1940s but was centered on Fazlur Khan's development of the framed-tube system for skyscraper design in the 1960s.

semidome: A half dome.

shear wall: A type of lateral bracing consisting of a reinforced concrete or masonry wall filling in one or more bays of the frame.

simply supported beam: A beam with one support at each end. These supports provide no resistance to rotation.

snow load: The weight of snow accumulating on a roof, bridge deck, or other surface.

space truss: A truss with a geometric configuration that can only be defined in 3-dimensional space, rather than a 2-dimensional plane.

spandrel: A triangular wall that fills in the space above an arch.

steel: A mixture of iron and carbon plus smaller amounts of other elements, such as manganese and chromium.

stiffening girder: A beam that directly supports the deck of a suspension bridge while resisting wind-induced vibration and distortion of the cable due to concentrated loads.

stiffening truss: A truss that directly supports the deck of a suspension bridge while resisting wind-induced vibration and distortion of the cable due to concentrated loads.

stiffness: A material's resistance to elastic deformation, measured as the slope of the lower (elastic) portion of the material's stress-strain curve.

strain: A dimensionless measure of the intensity of deformation.

strand: A bundle of parallel wires constituting a component of the main cable of a suspension bridge. Each cable is composed of multiple strands, and each strand is composed of multiple wires.

strand shoe: A horseshoe-shaped fitting that connects one strand of a suspension bridge cable to its anchorage.

strength: The largest stress a material can withstand before failing.

stress: The intensity of internal force measured in terms of force per unit area (e.g., pounds per square inch).

stress-strain curve: A graph of stress versus strain, used to characterize the engineering properties of a material.

structural system: An assembly of interconnected structural elements that transmits load from its point of application to the ground.

structure: The load-carrying elements of a building, bridge, or tower.

support: A physical connection between a structure and its surroundings.

suspended span: A central span of a cantilever bridge. The suspended span is supported by the cantilever arms.

suspender: A vertical cable that connects the stiffening truss or stiffening girder to a main cable in a suspension bridge.

suspension bridge: A structure in which the deck is supported on or beneath two or more draped cables.

tension: An internal force that causes a structural element to elongate.

tension member: A structural element that carries load primarily in tension (i.e., by elongating).

tension structure: A structural system in which most of the principal load-carrying elements are cables or membranes carrying load in tension.

tepidarium: The medium-temperature room in a Roman bath.

thin shell: A structural element that attains both strength and stability from its curved shape.

through truss: A truss bridge with the deck located at the level of the bottom chord.

thrust: The outward force exerted by an arch on its supports, caused by the tendency of an arch to spread outward under load.

thrust line: A graphical representation of the path of the internal compression force through a structural element.

tied arch: An arch in which the lateral thrust is resisted by a tension member connecting the 2 ends of the arch together.

timbrel vault: A thin-shell vault made of multiple layers of ceramic tile.

torsion: Twisting of a structural element.

traffic load: The weight of cars, trucks, trains, and other vehicles crossing a bridge.

traveler: A device used to fabricate suspension bridge cables in place on the bridge by pulling individual loops of wire across the span one at a time.

true arch: An arch constructed of wedge-shaped voussoirs, as distinguished from a corbelled arch.

truss: A structure consisting of elements arranged in interconnected triangles. These elements carry load primarily in tension or compression.

trussed-tube system: A variation on the framed-tube system. A trussed tube integrates diagonal braces into the exterior lateral load-carrying frame.

tryglyph: A rectangular architectural feature on the frieze of a Greek temple.

ultimate strength: The largest stress a material can withstand before it fractures in tension, measured as the height of the material's stress-strain curve.

velarium: A fabric awning that was stretched over the seating area of the Roman Colosseum to shade the spectators.

vertical: A vertically oriented truss member.

voussoir: A wedge-shaped element of an arch.

web: The vertical element of an I-shaped cross-section.

wind load: The pressure exerted by wind striking and flowing around a structure.

wrought iron: A construction material made by heating iron ore in a furnace and then beating it with a hammer or flattening it with heavy rollers to remove impurities and increase its ductility.

yielding: Material behavior characterized by large plastic deformations occurring with little or no increase in load. When a material yields, it begins to fail.

Bibliography

General References

Addis, Bill. *Building: 3000 Years of Design, Engineering and Construction.* London: Phaidon Press, 2007. A comprehensive and well-illustrated history of building design and construction, with emphasis on the evolution of engineering design and innovation.

American Society of Civil Engineers. *Minimum Design Loads for Buildings and Other Structures.* Reston, VA: American Society of Civil Engineers, 2002. A technical reference for the calculation of loads used in structural design.

Beckett, Derrick. *Great Buildings of the World: Bridges.* London: Hamlyn, 1969. A fine overview of the engineering design and construction of the Iron Bridge at Coalbrookdale, Telford's Menai Strait Bridge, Stephenson's Britannia Bridge, and Eiffel's Garabit Viaduct.

Billington, David P. *The Tower and the Bridge: The New Art of Structural Engineering.* Princeton, NJ: Princeton University Press, 1985. A thought-provoking analysis of noteworthy towers, bridges, and thin-shell structures that are both engineering marvels and, in Billington's view, works of art.

Buchholdt, H. A. *Introduction to Cable Roof Structures.* Cambridge: Cambridge University Press, 1985. A technical reference on the analysis of tension structures. Includes a good general overview of this unique structural form.

Burden, Ernest E. *Illustrated Dictionary of Architecture.* New York: McGraw Hill, 2002. A useful reference for terminology associated with architecture and structural engineering.

Cowan, Henry J., Ruth Greenstein, Bronwyn Hanna, John Haskell, Trevor Howells, Deborah Malor, John Phillips, Thomas Ranieri, Mark Stiles, and Bronwyn Sweeney. *The World's Greatest Buildings: Masterpieces in*

Architecture and Engineering. Sydney: Weldon Owen, 2000. A beautifully illustrated survey of 100 great buildings from antiquity to the present. Provides a description of each building but relatively little information on design and construction.

De Camp, L. Sprague. *The Ancient Engineers.* New York: Ballantine, 1963. A comprehensive history of the development of engineering and technology in the ancient, medieval, and early Renaissance eras.

Drysdale, Robert G., Ahmad A. Hamid, and Lawrie R. Baker. *Masonry Structures: Behavior and Design.* 2nd ed. Boulder: The Masonry Society, 1999. A technical reference on the analysis and design of masonry structures. Includes an excellent historical overview of the development of stone and brick masonry in the ancient world.

Dupré, Judith. *Bridges.* New York: Black Dog & Leventhal, 1997. An illustrated survey of the world's greatest bridges. The book's unusual format—18 inches wide by 8 inches high—accommodates long, narrow photographs of long-span structures.

————. *Skyscrapers.* New York: Black Dog & Leventhal, 1996. An illustrated survey of the world's greatest skyscrapers. The book's unusual format—8 inches wide by 18 inches high—accommodates tall, narrow photographs of skyscrapers.

Fanelli, Giovanni, and Michele Fanelli, *Brunelleschi's Cupola: Past and Present of an Architectural Masterpiece.* Florence, Italy: Mandragora, 2004. A detailed, scholarly analysis of the dome of the cathedral of Santa Maria del Fiore. Includes a modern structural analysis of the dome, as well as extensive information on Brunelleschi's construction techniques.

Favier, Jean. *The World of Chartres.* New York: Harry N. Abrams, 1990. A comprehensive and extensively illustrated description of the gothic cathedral at Chartres.

Gordon, J. E. *Structures: Or, Why Things Don't Fall Down*. New York: Da Capo, 1978. A well-written and entertaining introduction to engineering mechanics for nonengineers.

Hilson, Barry. *Basic Structural Behaviour: Understanding Structures from Models*. London: Thomas Telford, 1993. An introduction to structural analysis that uses simple physical models to illustrate concepts.

Humphrey, John W., John P. Oleson, and Andrew N. Sherwood. *Greek and Roman Technology: A Sourcebook*. London: Routledge, 1998. A comprehensive compilation of ancient source material relating to engineering and technology. Includes chapters on transport, construction, and metallurgy.

Landels, J. G. *Engineering in the Ancient World*. New York: Barnes & Noble, 1978. A short but engaging account of technological development in ancient Greece and Rome.

Levy, Matthys, and Mario Salvadori. *Why Buildings Fall Down*. New York: Norton, 1992. An introduction to structural engineering using case studies of structural failures to illustrate important concepts.

Macauley, David. *Building Big*. New York: Houghton Mifflin, 2000. The author's sketches illustrate how representative examples of great structures were built. Intended primarily for young people, this book is appropriate for all ages because of the unique clarity of its illustrations.

McCullough, David. *The Great Bridge*. New York: Simon & Schuster, 1972. A wonderfully written history of the design and construction of the Brooklyn Bridge.

Newhouse, Elizabeth L., ed. *The Builders: Marvels of Engineering*. Washington, DC: National Geographic Society, 1992. A beautifully illustrated summary of the world's great works of engineering.

Nilson, Arthur H., David Darwin, and Charles W. Dolan. *Design of Concrete Structures*. New York: McGraw-Hill, 2009. A technical reference on the design of reinforced concrete structural elements. Includes introductory information on types of modern concrete structures and concrete material properties.

Norwich, John J. *Great Architecture of the World*. London: Mitchell Beazley, 1975. An excellent compilation of the world's great buildings and towers, presented from an architectural perspective.

Nuttgens, Patrick. *The Story of Architecture*. 1st ed. Oxford: Phaidon, 1983. A comprehensive summary of architectural history.

Peters, Tom F. *Transitions in Engineering: Guillaume Henri Dufour and the Early 19th Century Cable Suspension Bridges*. Basel, Switzerland: Birkhäuser, 1987. A scholarly study of Dufour's development of the world's first wire-cable suspension bridge. Also provides excellent background on the first 50 years of modern suspension bridge design in the United States, Great Britain, and France.

Petroski, Henry. *Engineers of Dreams: Great Bridge Builders and the Spanning of America*. New York: Knopf, 1995. An engaging history of bridge building in the United States, with emphasis on the work of Eads, Cooper, Lindenthal, Moisseiff, and Ammann.

Riley, William F., Leroy D. Sturges, and Don H. Morris. *Statics and Mechanics of Materials: An Integrated Approach*. New York: John Wiley & Sons, 1995. An introductory textbook in engineering mechanics, with comprehensive coverage of forces, moments, equilibrium, stress, strain, and material properties.

Salvadori, Mario. *Why Buildings Stand Up: The Strength of Architecture*. New York: Norton, 1980. An excellent introduction to structural engineering using great structures to illustrate important concepts.

Sass, Stephen L. *The Substance of Civilization: Materials and Human History from the Stone Age to the Age of Silicon*. New York: Arcade, 1998. A fascinating history of engineering materials from antiquity to the present.

Smith, Bryan Stafford, and Alex Coull. *Tall Building Structures: Analysis and Design*. New York: Wiley, 1991. A technical reference on tall building design. Provides good background information on the types of structural systems used in skyscrapers.

Timoshenko, Stephen P. *History of Strength of Materials*. New York: McGraw Hill, 1953. An excellent overview of the historical development of engineering mechanics as a science.

Tzonis, Alexander. *Santiago Calatrava—The Complete Works*. Expanded ed. New York: Rizzoli, 2007. An extraordinarily beautiful compilation of photographs and descriptions of Calatrava's greatest buildings, bridges, and towers.

Van der Zee, John. *The Gate: The True Story of the Design and Construction of the Golden Gate Bridge*. New York: Simon & Schuster, 1986. An excellent history of the design, construction, and subsequent retrofit of the Golden Gate Bridge.

Winpenny, Thomas R. *Without Fitting, Filing, or Chipping: An Illustrated History of the Phoenix Bridge Company*. Easton, PA: Canal History and Technology Press, 1996. Provides descriptions of early pin-connected truss bridges and an excellent summary of the circumstances leading to the Quebec Bridge collapse from the perspective of the company that built the bridge.

Zarghamee, Mehdi S, Yasuo Kitane, Ömer O. Erbay, Therese P. McAllister, and John L. Gross. *Federal Building and Fire Safety Investigation of the World Trade Center Disaster: Global Structural Analysis of the Response of the World Trade Center Towers to Impact Damage and Fire*. National Institute of Standards and Technology Report NCSTAR 1-6D (September 2005). The technical report on the causes of the World Trade Center collapse.

Technical Reports and Specialty Publications

These specialty publications are not readily available, but they provided important and unique contributions to the course.

Ales, Joseph M., and Mark Waggoner. "Wide Open." *Civil Engineering* 73 (December 2003): 60–7. A description of the design and construction of the University of Phoenix Stadium.

Baker, William F., James J. Pawlikowski, and Bradley S. Young. "Reaching Toward the Heavens." *Civil Engineering* 80 (March 2010): 48–55. A description of the design and construction of the Burj Khalifa skyscraper.

Griggs, Francis E. "Squire Whipple—Father of Iron Bridges." *Journal of Bridge Engineering* 7 (May/June 2002): 146–55. An excellent summary of Squire Whipple's often overlooked contributions to structural engineering.

Mendelssohn, K. "A Building Disaster at the Meidum Pyramid." *The Journal of Egyptian Archaeology* 59 (August 1973): 60–71. Mendelssohn's analysis of the collapse of the Meidum Pyramid.

Pollalis, Spiro N., and Caroline Otto. "The Golden Gate Bridge: The 50th Anniversary Celebration." Harvard University Laboratory for Construction Technology Report LCT-88-4 (November 1988). Analysis of the bridge's response to pedestrian overloads during the 50th anniversary celebration.

Reid, Robert L. "Aerial Gateway." *Civil Engineering* 78 (October 2008): 42–51. A description of the newly constructed Terminal 3 at Beijing Capital International Airport.

Rondal, Jacques, and Kim Rasmussen. "On the Strength of Cast Iron Columns." *Journal of Constructional Steel Research* 60 (2004): 1257–70. Background information on the application of modern structural analysis methods to evaluate the strength of cast-iron columns in older structures.

Sadek, Fahim. "Baseline Structural Performance and Aircraft Impact Damage Analysis of the World Trade Center Towers." National Institute of Standards and Technology Report NCSTAR 1-2 (September 2005). The technical report summarizing the causes of the collapse of the World Trade Center on September 11, 2001.

Schober, Hans. "The Berlin Connection." *Civil Engineering* 76 (August 2006): 42–9. A description of the design and construction of the new Berlin Hauptbahnhof.

Spoth, Thomas, Ben Whisler, and Tim Moore. "Crossing the Narrows." *Civil Engineering* 78 (February 2008): 38–47. A description of the newly constructed suspension bridge across the Tacoma Narrows, with historical background on the failure of the original structure.

Weingardt, Richard G. "Anton Tedesko: Father of Thin-Shell Concrete Construction in America." *Structure* (April 2007): 69–71. An overview of Tedesco's contributions to thin-shell concrete construction in the United States.

Websites

Structurae. http://en.structurae.de/. An extensive database of the world's great structures. Provides photos and basic descriptive information about each structure as well as links to additional resources.

Historic American Buildings Survey/Historic American Engineering Record (HABS/HAER). http://memory.loc.gov/ammem/collections/habs_haer/. An extensive collection of photos, detailed descriptive information, and historical background on historically important American structures. The HABS and HAER collections are compiled by the National Parks Service and maintained by the Library of Congress.

Notes

Notes

Notes

Notes

Notes

Notes